New Jack

New Jack

Memoir of a Pro Wrestling Extremist

NEW JACK *and* JASON NORMAN

Foreword by Brian Heffron,
aka the Blue Meanie

McFarland & Company, Inc., Publishers
Jefferson, North Carolina

All photographs are from
Jerome "New Jack" Young's collection.

ISBN (print) 978-1-4766-7977-8
ISBN (ebook) 978-1-4766-3830-0

LIBRARY OF CONGRESS AND BRITISH LIBRARY
CATALOGUING DATA ARE AVAILABLE

Library of Congress Control Number 2019055238

On the cover: Pro wrestler New Jack (Jerome Young collection)

Printed in the United States of America

*McFarland & Company, Inc., Publishers
Box 611, Jefferson, North Carolina 28640
www.mcfarlandpub.com*

To my dad,
Samuel Young, Jr.

Table of Contents

Table of Contents

Foreword

New Jack probably doesn't remember either of the two times we've met.

When I was just starting out in wrestling, at any show, I always made it a tradition to introduce myself to everybody. I went down to a Smoky Mountain Wrestling show when I was training with Al Snow, and in Smoky Mountain they were still old school: they had the babyface locker room and the heel locker room, and the twain didn't meet, not until everyone was *far* from the arena!

I went to the heel locker room and met Jack. He was nice, but you could tell he was guarded. I was this *new* kid, in *his* locker room. But he was cool. I made sure not to say too much and got out fast.

In Smoky Mountain, less was more. You'd see the Gangstas working as heels, but you could tell they were having fun; I saw a tag match where the Gangstas faced Boo Bradley (later to wind up as Balls Mahoney in ECW) and Boo would do a dance. I'd see them trying not to laugh. It's one reason why so many people had a lot of respect for New Jack long before he went to ECW.

He was in ECW before I showed up there, and I didn't think he'd remember me. He didn't, but I went right back up and introduced myself. I learned fast that he was a good dude. I was hoping he felt the same way about me; early on in my ECW career, I was in a tag match with Chad Austin and the Gangstas, and I found out I was right. Wait until you get to *that* chapter in this book!

After shows at the ECW Arena, things just turned into one big party between the wrestlers and our fans. People were around New Jack all the time; I remember once a fan came up to Jack and told him he wanted to be a wrestler. Jack gave him all kinds of advice on what to do, how to train, how to lose weight. It was something special to help someone who wanted to get into the wrestling business. I don't know if that guy ever did, but if so, I hope he gives New Jack some credit.

Foreword by Brian "The Blue Meanie" Heffron

I worked with New Jack a lot, and I always felt safe. A lot of people looked at New Jack, and ECW wrestlers in general, as guys who like to shoot on each other. That's the farthest thing from the truth. Jack always protected me, never forced anything. There were plenty of times when he'd

ask me if I wanted to do something. He was always OK with me saying no.

People know him as a controversial guy, and, yes, he says a lot of things to get a rise out of people. You put him with a microphone, and it's like listening to a great preacher during a religious experience. But one-on-one, you get to know New Jack, and you get to know Jerome.

The persona, the person—they're both pretty cool. After reading this book, I think you'll feel the same about the two.

—Brian "The Blue Meanie" Heffron

Brian Heffron, a.k.a. The Blue Meanie, became one of the most recognizable figures in the squared circle during his time with Extreme Championship Wrestling and the World Wrestling Federation (later World Wrestling Entertainment) in the 1990s and early 2000s.

Introduction

Millions of people had seen it on pay-per-view. Thousands of people went insane in the stands in that Connecticut town.

And there I'd lie, in the middle of it all, not being able to see or hear a thing.

Now, weeks later, I laid in a room upstairs at a friend's house, listening to a TV I couldn't see. It could have been noon or midnight or anything in between—I couldn't tell.

My wrestling career was over. I knew it. Anyone who'd watched ECW's *Living Dangerously* had seen it. I'd felt it.

Now I was trying to decide if everything should end right then and there. Not just my career, but my entire life.

The story of New Jack the wrestler had rambled through one explosive chapter after another. Maybe it was time for the story to end. Extreme wrestling had been my life for nearly a decade. Maybe it was supposed to be my way out.

I'd broken bones and lost teeth before. Big deal, right? You don't get into wrestling, particularly Extreme Championship Wrestling, and think you're not going to get hurt. You expect it. Sometimes if I got through a match *without* feeling it hard, I'd be disappointed in myself.

I got hurt all the time—but New Jack didn't. He was a guy who always got back up and went back in to battle. He got hit with everything in the world, he got smashed through tables, he got crushed by guys twice his size. Then he'd get back up and dare the opponents to come back and do it again. He'd get on the mic and let people know he was still around and still out for more. He'd get beaten up and beaten down, but never taken out. He'd take punishment that had put bigger guys into early retirement and do even worse the next day.

But the guy behind him was, well, a little more human. That's what wrestling fans—even today, with websites and dirt sheets blaring out all the backstage garbage that informs those who yell about how "fake" wrestling is—don't realize or remember.

Introduction

I was doing it because I was having fun. I was willing to go to the extreme when I did my shit. Diving off balconies and scaffolds, getting cut up—I did it because it was there. Now I'd gotten hurt worse than ever. And being New Jack in front of the crowds wasn't going to bail me out.

The plan had been for Vic Grimes and I to fall off the scaffold, crash through a few tables, then land on the concrete floor of the O'Neil Center in Danbury. Then we'd get up and keep fighting.

Simple, right? To the ECW crew, it was everyday stuff.

Even with such specifics, though, something had gone wrong. I'd hit the floor, and Grimes had landed right on my head, driving it straight into the concrete. My head had burst open, spitting out blood, brain fluid, everything.

I'd laid there and had a seizure right in the middle of a show. At least, that's what I heard and saw later on the tapes; I'd been a hundred feet past consciousness at the time.

Then I was stretchered out, spent a week in the hospital, and, somehow, been released. Not that I knew what the hell was going on through any of it.

I couldn't see. That blow to the brain might have knocked my sight out permanently. Even the doctors didn't know what would happen. I'd had an MRI, and there was a crack behind my left ear over two inches long.

A friend of mine down in Atlanta had taken me in. Then I lost it.

I'd never be able to wrestle again. What the hell are you supposed to think when your sight suddenly disappears, and your skull might be permanently busted open? What would I ever be able to do again at all?

Nothing. Except this.

I was ready to end everything. If my friends hadn't hidden all the guns and knives in the home, I probably would have.

It wasn't safe for me to leave the top floor; I'd tried, and fallen down the stairs. I was stuck recording an *Andy Griffith Show* marathon and sitting there every day in the dark, just listening to it. My friends made sure I got enough to eat, and eventually they took me outside, but I still couldn't tell if it was night or day.

They even called my mother and told her what was going on. Typical for her, she said she couldn't afford to come see me. Just what I expected.

There was nothing to do but wait. Like every wrestler, I'd been on the go for years, bouncing all over the place from city to city and show to show, and now I couldn't do anything but sit there and hope my body would heal itself.

Way too slowly, my sight began to come back. Things got blurry as hell, then more focused.

On the left side, at least. Even today, nearly two decades later, I still have only about five percent of sight in my right eye.

ECW head man Paul Heyman, the guy who'd come up with the original idea for Grimes and I to come crashing down, finally called me.

"I want to come back," I vowed to him. He couldn't believe it. He asked me if I was sure. How could anyone go through this and want some more?

I was sure. My sight was coming back. Now I'd be back.

My friends had told me to quit. My doctors just assumed I would. Even if my eyes got better—a huge fucking if—my skull would never totally heal. Even today, it's still sensitive to the touch, and I've tempted fate far more times than I ever should have. People had been doubting New Jack's mental stability for years, and now I'd give them an even better reason to feel that way.

I couldn't get hurt any worse. If I did, I'd probably die right there in the ring. If that was my fate, New Jack's destiny, I was OK with it because I was settling the score with a guy who'd never called me during the time I'd been out—the guy who'd put me there to begin with.

Wrestling's a weird business. It's one where the rules of everyday society don't come anywhere near application. In wrestling, it's pretty normal to bash a guy's head in with a chair, throw him through a table, have him slam your head into the concrete floor, and a week later be his friend and tag team partner if a new enemy comes around.

Who in the hell would ever do this? How could you be friends with someone who did something that, if done outside the ring, would be a felony, and who then did it again the next week? It's one of the strangest parts of a business where normalcy never happens.

Time passes quickly for wrestling fans, but those recovery weeks seemed like years, decades—for me, even forever.

I was coming back. Just over two months after I almost died (a few times over!), I walked into the Rave in Milwaukee, ready to go some more. Ready to show that New Jack was more than just not human— he was indestructible. Ready to send certain people to Hardcore Heaven.

As Grimes and his buddies in Da Baldies ganged up on their opponents after their match, I came storming out, ready to kick ass in the realest sense.

I'd never been too safe in the ring, at least not to myself. I wasn't starting now. With Grimes's pal Tony DeVito sprawled on a table, I smashed right through him. From a balcony. The fans were shocked, but probably not surprised.

I came crashing down on the other baldy, Angel, from the top, helped along with all kinds of other foreign objects that were always typical in ECW.

The move is called the 187, named after cop jargon for murder. If I got Grimes in the ring, I might have caused the real thing.

But for now, New Jack was back, motherfucker. And he'd be around a while.

Fortunately, so would Jerome Young, the man behind New Jack. It got to the point over the years that it became weird for me to be called Jerome or Mr. Young or anything but New Jack. No one really knew the guy that so many know of, not even those that had hit the mat with me, and hit me with everything but a tank.

Now they will. Over the next few thousand words, New Jack and Jerome will tell more than anyone ever knew, more than anyone ever thought existed between the man outside the curtain and the one who'd suffered in that sad attic for the first part of 2000.

See, when you go to another company, you're sort of starting over. You try not to assume that fans will remember your past issues with people. They know you and your persona, but not really your past feuds. You're starting fresh.

But not me. I didn't give a damn who recalled what Grimes and I had been through, and who didn't have a clue why I was pissed. If I had to follow him out of ECW and somewhere else, chase him for years, I was going to have my revenge, as both New Jack and Jerome.

It would still be some time before I got my hands back on Grimes. But I'd be ready.

1

Growing Up Violent

If it's all you know, all you experience almost every day, you think it's normal. You think that everyone grows up this way, that it's just the way things are. Every kid goes through that for his first few years, before he's out in the world, getting to know people, going to kindergarten and finding out how the rest of the world works.

Violence has been a part of my life since before I can remember. I'm the youngest of five kids, so it didn't start with me, and the first time I can recall definitely wasn't the first time it occurred in the Young household of Greensboro, North Carolina, in the late 1960s.

I was about five years old, and my parents were having their usual screaming match. They fought crazy fights up and down, all over the house, everywhere. Yelling, cursing, hitting—it was all everyday stuff to me.

Someone had called my dad and told him that my mom was seen in a car with another man. She'd denied it, and he didn't believe her.

They yelled, they cursed, they accused, they threatened. I didn't do much. What was I supposed to do? I was five years old! Who would listen to a kindergartner? I just sat around and watched, like it was another TV show or something. It had happened before, and I was pretty sure it would end soon, at least for the time being. This sort of thing was always starting and stopping in our place.

It kept going. But this time, things got worse, and almost ended for the last time.

My dad took a knife, which he always carried, and started waving it at my mom, moving toward her with the whole family watching. She was screaming at him, telling him to put it away, that she hadn't done anything wrong.

It didn't work. He started stabbing her. One, two, three, four, five times, in the chest, the stomach, all over her body. We all just sat there and watched, shaking our heads like it was no big deal. It was worse than we'd ever seen before, but not so much that we were taken aback.

Somehow, she got away and called the police. They took my dad away, and my mom went to the hospital. One of her lungs collapsed, and they thought she wasn't going to make it. But she did, and got back home.

And so did my dad. He was in and out of jail fast. That civil rights stuff had been going on for years, but we were still below the Mason-Dixon Line, and no one, not even the law (*especially* not the law) gave a shit about black-on-black crime. Go at a white person and there was hell to pay. Keep it within the black race and they did everything but encourage it. Nobody was going to put a black man in jail for hurting a black woman.

Dad came home, and Mom stayed. That was just how things went back then. I knew things would happen again, and it didn't bother me. Because, again, as far as I knew, every house in Greensboro, let alone the rest of America, lived the same way I did. I could go north or south or anywhere else and every husband and wife would be doing this, every kid would be seeing it. I didn't really live in a violent neighborhood, but the household was more than enough.

I was living that way before I was even old enough for kindergarten, and so was my family. The fighting kept going. One day, my mother had had enough. She grabbed me and a bunch of her stuff and took everything out to the car. My father wasn't having it. He barreled right out after her.

"You ain't taking my son!," he raged (my siblings all had different dads, so he and I were closer than they were to him). "Put my son down!" You didn't take things that belonged to him, no matter how he treated them.

She opened the door and bent over to put me in the backseat. Then I heard a loud noise, and she let me go, turned, and grabbed her leg.

My father was holding a gun. He'd put a bullet in her.

Again, she escaped and called the police. Again, she went to the hospital, and he to the jail. And again, he was in and out and back home soon.

This time, it didn't last as long, but not for the reasons you'd expect.

My dad, I thought, was basically a pretty cool guy. He drove a truck around to put down asphalt. He drove people around in a cab. Sometimes he'd bring me along, and I thought his work was fun. I had a much better relationship with him than with my mom. She was mean, yelling at me and my siblings, taking out the problems she'd had with my dad on us.

Remember, back then, I'd seen and heard the violence so much in my life that I didn't think it was wrong. It was just something people did, something everyone did. It's taken me a long time to realize the other side of that, and I don't think I ever will completely understand.

1. Growing Up Violent

Many people badmouthed my family, still do. They looked down on me and my siblings for the way we acted back then. I'll bet you that those people weren't raised like we were. They didn't see what we did or go through the things we went through, with such different ideas about right and wrong.

One day not long after the shooting, before my sixth birthday, I was out riding my bike. Someone came out of my house and called me to come in.

My father had been to the hospital recently, and all they told me was that his chest was hurting. I was a little kid, what did I know? You hurt a little, you get better, you move on.

Then I went inside and got the news no kid should ever hear, no matter what kind of parents he has. They'd gotten a phone call that my father had suddenly dropped dead of a heart attack. I don't remember where he was or too much about it. All I knew then was that my dad was gone. At five years old, you don't have the mind to know or care about things like circumstances. You just know that a guy you just saw, someone who was as decent a fellow as I could tell, wasn't ever coming back.

That's right around the time that things got worse between my mom and I, and they've never been good. Still aren't. After my dad died, she'd bring men over, and I'd be in the next room, trying to sleep, listening to her have sex. She never supported me, never came to my football games, let alone my wrestling matches. Her reaction to my injuries in the Grimes match sadly wasn't a surprise.

My dad is buried in Greensboro, right near my grandmother and a cousin. I still go by and check on their graves sometimes.

People have asked what qualities of his I carry on, if there's anything I try to instill in my family, my children, that he showed me. I think every man is expected to hold on to a part of his father, particularly when he himself becomes a dad.

They're usually unpleasantly surprised when I tell them.

First off, my dad was a drinker. A *heavy* drinker. That's another thing that I thought was normal growing up. People who didn't drink, man, what was up with them? It was just something you're supposed to do.

I did that. I guess it gave me an advantage in wrestling. Lots of wrestlers drink their way through the pain and loneliness that come from getting slammed all over the ring for a night, then having to do it again and again until you're lucky enough to get hurt and take time off. Most people don't start it until they're well into the business. I was too well acquainted with it before I even began. I still like to throw back a few, and then a few more.

The second part was that my dad always carried a knife. A *big fucking knife*. Whatever he needed it for, it was his prized possession. I do as well.

And wrestling wasn't the first time I'd get the place to use it.

2

Moving Everywhere

If there was one thing consistent about my upbringing, it's that it was always changing. My family and I would get settled somewhere, and a few months later, we'd be out of there. It was nothing unusual to come home and have my mother throw up her hands and blare, "I hate this place! Get your shit and get packed. Fuck this, we're moving."

I was always like, "Fuck, here we go again with this shit." But I made her pay; she'd be coming home from work one day, and I'd climb up on top of the house and jump in front of her car—actually a much shorter leap than the ones I'd be taking decades later in ECW!

She, of course, would get out and beat the shit out of me, calling me a crazy little fucker. I always thought it was funny.

We moved all over the place. In twelve years, I went to twelve different schools. I was at six different schools through sixth grade in North Carolina, then went down to Atlanta and hit a bunch of schools down there.

But I somehow managed to keep my grades pretty high, even with getting new teachers and classmates every year. Some were tougher than others, but I don't think I ever had an easy time.

All my young life, I was adjusting to another constantly changing set of acquaintances—the football coaches and teammates I was always playing for. I'd picked up the gridiron game. Wiry and fast, I was shutting down receivers all over the field, like my main NFL man Lester Hayes was doing for the Oakland Raiders at that point.

That speed came from running the 4 × 400 in track and playing soccer. And, yes, I also wrestled at one of my high schools. But I wasn't really into it. I basically only did it because my football coach recommended it. I did OK, not great, but it sure got me into better shape.

And I'd have to be physically fit for my run-ins with the justice system.

Heading out of school one day in my junior year, my friends came and grabbed me. They looked pissed off like I'd never seen before. Were we about to get into a battle royal long before wrestling?

No—some scumbag had jumped on my girlfriend and used her as a punching bag. That shit wasn't happening. I hopped in my car and followed his bus. We pulled up to a shopping center, and he got out and started walking across the lot. Wide open. Easy target.

I pulled in slowly and got him in my sights over the hood. Then I hit the gas hard. This guy was going to be Atlanta's largest piece of roadkill.

Just in time, he turned and saw me. He jumped out of the way with centimeters to spare.

But there was a Plan B. I came flying out of the car, and we started beating the hell out of each other. This fight wasn't going to end with pinfall or submission.

No, just with outside interference. The cops showed up, pulled us apart, and tossed both of us in the back of their cars.

I only spent one night in jail. It wasn't on school property, so the school didn't give a shit.

At this time, I look back and think it's funny, or at least ironic. Pro wrestling was on TV, but I didn't care much for it. I think I knew who Dusty Rhodes was, but I wouldn't have recognized him if he'd walked past me. Wrestling wasn't a part of my life, even as a fan, and it wouldn't be for a long time. Besides, I had more than enough to worry about.

One more year, one more school. My last year, I headed to DM Therrell High School for my farewell senior tour.

I was back on one more football team, and we kicked some serious ass. Fans and classmates came to see me. I'd end up on the school's Wikipedia page, so someone must still be proud of and remember me!

Then scouts started following us. The University of North Carolina wanted me to come and play. So did A&T University.

Still today, people dangle college in students' eyes as "your ticket out of here and to success! It's a great way to fame and fortune!" I agree with their reasons for doing that; most kids today, especially black kids without fathers or much of a chance, like I was, need to hear that message. But it wasn't really my main attraction to further education.

I wasn't really looking forward to college for academic reasons, although I did hope it would help me become a physical education teacher. It wasn't even football. Of course, I'd have loved to have gotten a shot at the NCAA and eventually the NFL, but that wasn't it.

For me, it was more about stability. No matter where I ended up, I'd be in the same place for a while for the first time. No mother on my back, yanking the rug out from under me when she got restless. I'd be in the

Football was a huge part of my life for years—I always thought it would be my most physical athletic pastime.

same place long enough to at least *focus*. Maybe make some *lasting relationships*. Maybe *know people and places for a while*.

Unfortunately, it was never meant to be. See, I had already started to fuck everything up—and when everyone found out, it all came crashing down.

3

Recording Some Crime

By the second half of my senior year, I was doing all kinds of things that I hoped no one would ever learn about. Between track meets and soccer games, I was going out with my buddies almost every weekend.

So what, right? Lots of guys do that. We go out, raise a little hell, get into trouble once in a while, masculinity over maturity. What teenage boys don't?

We liked to party, and everyone was aware of that. Every high school has a few fellows with a reputation, but no worse than anyone else. Yeah, we were the same pains in the ass that every teenage boy is sometimes, but, again, nothing new or unusual.

But no one knew what we really did. Joyriding, staying out until all hours, yes. But for the first few months of 1981, we'd picked up some much worse practices.

Almost every weekend, it wasn't unusual for us to roar into a 7-Eleven, a sporting goods store, whatever else, and walk out with more than we came in with. Only we didn't pay. We took without buying, or asking.

When we walked into class on Monday mornings all dressed alike, it was a sign that many probably picked up on, but no one ever mentioned. It was because we'd been out robbing and stealing, and then spent the take at the mall.

We had a routine, a few of us. We'd pull up to a store and jump out of the car. One of us would have a gun. Then we'd go in, scare the hell out of everyone, and roll out. But that's all we did at first: frighten. We charged through weekends' worth of criminal activity without hurting anyone.

Until the last time.

My friends and I were sitting around, when one of us (I hope it wasn't me!) mentioned that we should go rob a jewelry store. We figured another simple in-and-out deal, maybe with some goods that we could pawn, or maybe use to score a few points by giving them to some local lovelies!

That's how it started out. We went in, and it was me holding the gun.

I pointed it straight at the clerk and let him know that it was the goods or his life.

He emptied out the register. He dumped all the jewelry on the counter. This was how it had always gone.

Then, for some reason that, even nearly three decades later, I don't even comprehend, I decided to hit him. I smashed him in the head with the gun.

He went down, and we went out, thinking we were going to get away again.

Not this time. Security cameras weren't as widespread then as they are today, but this place had them. They got the car, the license plate, everything, on tape. It took the cops about five minutes to find out whose car it was, and things went pretty smoothly for them from there.

The next weekend, I was out of town. When I got back, I saw one of my robbing buddies walking out of my apartment complex, a scared look on his face. He didn't say hello to me, and I thought that was strange.

I got back to my apartment, and my mother's boyfriend was there. He'd never trusted or liked me, and that feeling was mutual, but there were more important things at work here.

"The police are looking for you, Jerome," he said gravely. Oh shit.

"For what?" I asked, like I didn't know. His eyes narrowed. He sure as hell knew.

"Jerome," he said, in that way people do when they know you're full of it. "For that jewelry store you robbed."

My mother looked at me. "Did you do it?" she asked. Of course, she knew as well.

I couldn't even hesitate. "Yeah."

She took me downtown, and I turned myself in at the county jail. I didn't know what to think; I just knew that this wasn't like my high school "incarceration." I wasn't going to be walking away from this, not right away. All the crimes we'd gotten away with, and the one time that someone gets hurt, we get caught.

Up to that point, I'd expected my main June event to be walking out of Therrell with a mortarboard and kicking back for my last summer before full-blown adulthood. Instead, while so many of my friends were enjoying such a luxury, I was pleading guilty to armed robbery. Unsurprisingly, all my scholarship offers vanished.

Probably because I'd been pretty clean to that point, I got a zip-six, criminal jargon for a term between no time (yeah, right!) and six years.

If I'd been charged for all the robberies of which I'd been a part, I might never have become New Jack.

We headed down to the diagnostic center in Jackson, then to Alto State Prison right off of scenic Gainesville Highway (unfortunately, it didn't become an all-ladies place until more than twenty years later!).

With no real idea of how the hell I'd gotten myself here or what the hell I was supposed to do, I slumped down across from a counselor.

He told me I was getting a twenty-four-month contract. Yeah, they called it a "contract," like I was a big free agent with teams fighting over me. I'd be there for two years. Unless I got in trouble, in which case my residency would be lengthened. Basically, my contract could be extended without my consent. But if I stayed clear, I could get to a halfway house before doing the full term.

Maybe it was fate, making my stupid ass pay for hurting a guy who'd done everything I'd demanded.

The whole time in there, and even once in a while still, I think about what could have gone differently. Yes, of course I wish we'd never gone to that store. Of course, I wish I hadn't hit the man. But what if I'd hit him too hard, or in a different, more dangerous place? What if the gun had gone off when it hit him, or when I swung it? Someone could have been shot. Someone, maybe me or him or one of my friends, could have been killed.

And why? Just so my friends and I could have some fun and nice clothes? As you'll have figured out by the end of this book, if you haven't by now, I don't have many regrets. I'm not sorry for very much. But for that, I always will be.

But sorrow and regret and remorse don't get you anywhere in jail, and they can drive you nuts, another state that's way too easy to find in the clink. No cells here—we were in a dorm. Sometimes I'd wake up, and just think, why am I here? Then somebody would walk by, and I'd just run up and hit them. You get angry and frustrated, and if you take it out on anyone, you just get more to carry around.

I saw it all the time. People fought over *anything*. Stuff would get stolen, and no one was going to confess. Guys would get their trays knocked over, their snacks stolen, someone walking by could look at them wrong, and suddenly you'd see a dozen guys comparing fist strength and speed.

But I never got in too much trouble. I'd always manage to slip away before the fights I started got too out of hand, and no one tried to make me their good little girlfriend, something else I saw way too often. Guys in prison know who to fuck with and who not to, and I was in the gym every morning benching about 460 pounds. Seeing that convinced the "veterans" that there were other guys to prey on.

They found others to prag (sexually assault), and I burned calories in the morning and dinners in the evening cafeteria. Just before Thanksgiving of 1982, I vacated to a halfway house in Savannah.

Yes, this was the early 1980s, and America wasn't in the best shape, with the economy and everything else. Still, things didn't move forward as fast as the Internet and the rest of society hauls today. The world wasn't *that* different as it had been when I went in.

We spent our first month at the house learning to readjust, to stay the hell out. We talked about what to do and not to do, and then went back to our rooms. A few weeks in, we went on the job hunt, and I was back in the kitchen, this time at a local restaurant.

Financial smarts aren't too common among the ex-cons, so that's a big part of the halfway house, too. You get paid and bring your check back to the place. They give you about $20 a week and keep the rest, giving you some pittances for food allowances and rent. But if you make it through the longest six months since, well, since you were sentenced to begin with, you're released again. And in April 1983, with a few bucks and a bus ticket, I was a free man again, with a whole new set of chances.

Stepping onto that bus, all I could see was the future.

I was going back to Atlanta. I was going home.

I had no fucking clue where I was going at all.

4

Higher Education

Back in Atlanta, back with my mom. Some things had changed, but not many, and not really for the better.

My mom was still tough to be around. She still had a pretty bad taste in men. The guy she was with now used to fight with her all the time, and then he'd gotten into shit with me. One of my last going-away presents before I'd been to jail was yet another brawl with him, but he'd remember this one well.

We were in a fistfight, bodies and punches flying all over the place. Then he went for my throat and my face. He might have been trying to smother me, break my nose, gouge my eyes out.

The point is, he didn't get to do any of it. His fingers got near my mouth, and I latched onto one with all the force I could clamp down. I felt the meat in his hand giving way, and the disgusting taste of blood along with it. He got his hand away from my mouth, but left the tip of his middle finger behind. I'll bet he never forgets that one.

Well, I was on probation, so I had to get some things done. I went to work at a cement company in the mornings, then enrolled at Atlanta's Clark College (it became Clark Atlanta University a few years later). I got an apartment, and started majoring in physical education. Maybe I could convince certain people that I was a changed man.

I thought football might help. I got back on Clark's football team, and wowed the hell out of everybody. I guess a two-year layoff didn't hurt me too much.

We did really well, and scouts even started to show. One day, we went to a mini-camp tryout with the Atlanta Falcons; considering they had all of two winning seasons in the 1980s, we thought they'd be desperate for help.

I didn't get picked. But by then, I really wasn't thinking about school.

Most people go to college to get an education, get a degree, find some direction in their life. Me, it was just a way to stay out of jail. I went to class, I studied, I played football. But I was just doing it to make time hurry up and pass. I was never going to be a student, a career guy. Looking at New Jack in the ring, can you possibly imagine me proudly waving my diploma as "Pomp and Circumstance" was blaring?

No way. Like most people, I couldn't wait to finish college, but not because I wanted to take my degree and take over the world. I was there because it was that or back to jail. As those two long years wound down, I didn't know quite where I wanted to be, but it certainly wasn't there.

In the spring of 1986, I stepped away, ready to find the next part of Jerome Young. Jail hadn't worked for me. College hadn't given me the answer. It was time to find something else. And as luck would have it in the arrival of an old friend of mine, I did.

See, as dangerous as wrestling would ever be for me later on, what happened next would pale it in comparison. Because in my new career my life would be in danger every day. There was no predetermined outcome, nothing worked out with my opponents. The objects and ring weaponry that New Jack used to abuse his adversaries, and the ones they used on him, would be tame compared to what I'd see all too often over the next few years.

5

Hunting for Bounties

With no diploma to brag about and that black spot on my criminal past forever, it would be tough to get someone to see me as a long-term investment, even with the millions of people and tons of businesses all over good ol' Atlanta.

But an old friend did. He'd been in the bail bondsman business for a while, chasing down people who'd gotten lost on their way to court. I'd been on the wrong side of the law for too long; he thought I'd like to take it out on others who'd gone even farther bad.

He asked if I wanted to be a bounty hunter.

What? Was he crazy? I was a convicted felon, so I couldn't carry a gun. He thought I'd want to go after people even the cops couldn't even bring in? People who'd assaulted, raped, even killed? People who wouldn't think twice about taking my life to keep from heading back to the slammer? And even if I turned out to be good at it, I was bound to slip up somewhere. I might hit someone too hard, take them to the ground, anything that could get me right back into legal trouble. It's tough to imagine a less attractive career for a guy so recently off parole.

I said yes.

There was the money: catching the crooks would net me a percentage of the bond, and sometimes they can get pretty high. But basically, I just thought it would be interesting—and how right I was.

It was my very first "hunt." My first chase.

My buddy and I were sitting in a car one cold night in Atlanta. A bus pulled up down the street, and a man got off.

I saw my colleague's eyes widen, then focus. Our prey had arrived. This guy had skipped a court date, and managed to elude the fuzz.

"That's him," my friend swore.

"You sure?" I asked. "You sure that's him?"

"That's him," he repeated. "Let's wait for him to go to his apartment, and then we'll go and get him."

That would have been the safe thing to do. That would have been the smart thing. But it wasn't my thing. Maybe it was my naturally impulsive personality, which millions would soon see when New Jack arrived. Or maybe I just wanted to make an impression on my first night on the job.

The next thing my partner knew, he was alone in the car, and my door was wide open. I was running up the street like I was racing a cheetah.

I tackled the guy and slammed him to the ground.

"I ain't got no money!" he cried out. He thought that he was getting mugged and robbed. Foolish criminal.

"I don't want your money, motherfucker," I diplomatically explained. "You're going to jail." To that point, it was the most satisfying fifty dollars I'd ever made.

My co-workers seemed to think it was funny at the time, but I'd spend the next six months staying safely (for both me and the crooks) behind walls, writing up bonds and letting others do the hunting.

I was hooked. This was how I'd spend the rest of my life. But either I wasn't writing well enough, or my cutthroat approach had impressed some people, because by early 1987 I was back on the hunt.

Once we learned that a lady (who'd once played keyboard behind Isaac Hayes) had jumped bond, so we headed up to Memphis to get her. Her boyfriend, who'd been in the film *The Blues Brothers*, tried to help her out.

"You give us some time," he pleaded, "we can get you the bail money so she won't have to go to jail."

"I got a warrant, so I have to take her to Atlanta," I told him. "But here's what you can do."

As we arrived in Atlanta, my pager went off. They'd paid the money.

With the lady in her pajamas, I took her to the nearest Greyhound station, bought her a ticket, and sent her back home.

Yeah, I still got into some trouble. One time, we tracked a guy all the way to Amarillo, Texas. With my hand in his door, he slammed it, and I kicked it open, whooped his ass, and took him back to Atlanta.

Then I had to go back to Texas, get charged with aggravated assault, see it dropped down to property damage, and pay a small fine. Heading back and forth halfway across the country a few times over a broken door.

Like I said, I couldn't carry a gun, but damned if I was going out there naked. I had a knife, and I once had to put it into a guy who attacked me. I had to beat the shit out of a few people, and sometimes I got just as bad as I gave. That wasn't going to stop me. I've long accepted that violence is going to follow me for my entire life—and sometimes I've tried to make sure it keeps up.

There's tons of rumors all over the Internet about me, and some of them are pretty true. Maybe I've even started a few of those, with a little addition to the truth.

One is that I literally left bodies behind in my bounty-hunting career. That wasn't the case. I ensured that a few of the guys I caught had to visit the hospital before booking, but I didn't take any lives.

There were times, though, that I wished I could have. In late 1990 or early 1991, my partner and I were trying to grab a guy in Atlanta. He pulled a gun and tried to send us to eternity. I'd have put his ass there in a second if I'd been armed. Fortunately, my colleague was, and he ended the guy's criminal career with a well-placed shot. I helped with my knife.

That's the only death I've ever contributed to. Rumors of me taking other lives and getting away might have been overblown.

We had to go to court because of that, but it was dropped. Come to think of it, I got a few breaks from the justice system over my decade in that line of work. Enough that I started using them to my advantage when I branched off into a new line of work as the new decade began.

Not wrestling, not yet. That didn't start until 1992, and even then, it would take quite a bit more time before I'd get anywhere close to earning a living in the business. Very few people ever do, so I guess I'm lucky in that sense. I'm even luckier that no one I ever arrested and/or beat down in my career ever came back after me, at least not yet.

But, yes, almost no wrestler outside of the WWE (or TNA, to an extent) lives on his/her wrestler salary alone, and if they do, they're *hardly* scraping by. I'd stay with bounty hunting until I was at least in wrestling's minor leagues, but by then I was in a new, occasionally lucrative business—one that would have bounty hunters looking for me.

6

Drugs Arrive

Right around the first of the '90s, the same guy who'd gotten me started in the bounty business got a new idea to make some money. We'd been doing some dirty work on behalf of the law for a while now. Maybe we could use that to a little extra, though not entirely fair, advantage for ourselves.

He laid out the entire plan. He offered me some very generous compensation. Then I went down to Atlanta for my next pick up. Not to bring in a crook. This time, I'd be the criminal.

It was for drugs. I'd just kicked off my new source of income.

It's crazy to think about this sometimes, but I couldn't believe how easy it was to find and keep connections for this stuff. You ask around, you're going to meet people with the demand and the green to back it up, and you happily become the supply. You go to bars, up and down the streets, to the strip clubs. You find buyers, some all too happy to help you with the word of mouth that traffickers don't always want getting around. But you find people willing to buy, and they're handing over so much fucking money you don't worry about where they got it from.

You don't worry about the effects that your product could have, not after a while. If people don't get it from you, they'll get it from someone else. It's not your fault if they overdo it—and even considering how many return customers I had during those years, I don't believe any of my people ever snorted or smoked or shot up too much. If they had, that might have hurt my sales. Never happened.

Powder became my biggest asset. But not in the using sense. That would come *years* later.

I had a reliable supplier, and I kept up my sales prowess. If your customer service doesn't work in this business, people don't report you to the Better Business Bureau. They stomp you into the pavement, or put you six feet in the dirt. I was buying for dimes and selling for dollars. It's how any enterprising drug dealer gets ahead and stays ahead.

23

Sometimes, I brought my businesses together. If I needed to go to another city to get a shipment, I'd just find someone with an active warrant in that area, show up in my capacity as a bounty hunter, put him in handcuffs, go pick up the drugs and head right back.

Once I had to go all the way to Florida to get a couple of kilos, and made damn sure I had a fugitive in the car with me. If I got stopped, they could run his photo, and it would come up valid. I even called the state patrol to let them know what car I was driving, and the whole way home, I had cops waving me on as I headed by with two kilos of drugs in the trunk!

And it didn't stop when I got into wrestling. When I started out in Smoky Mountain Wrestling, I was still selling—not to the wrestlers, but to people I knew. One night, one of my customers called me, very soon after we'd done a deal.

"I was sitting here getting high," he reported, "and now I'm watching you here on TV! You're probably the only person I know who's on TV—legally!—after selling drugs." I kept it up for a few years after that, even for a while after I got to ECW. In 1994, I paid cash for a brand new Corvette, and I'm sure that probably got some people suspicious about my income, but no one wanted to ask any questions.

That's not to say I didn't have some close calls. With a pretty good money deal in place, I once flew all the way out to Houston to pick up a few very special kilos. Pulling into the hotel, I was already a little nervous—our room was on the backside of the building, making it tough to see.

Getting ready to check in, I called the guy to tell him I was ready to buy and bolt. This far from home, in this kind of game, you don't worry about getting to know people. He told me he'd be there tomorrow, it being a holiday.

Red flags went all the way up all over my mind. There's no such thing as a holiday in drug selling. Cops and detectives don't take time off to celebrate, so those on the other side don't either. You either have the money then and there or you don't have it at all. Drug dealers don't deal in IOUs.

I left the hotel, and went across the street to another place. Over there, I was looking out the window at our old place.

That night, a car pulled up, and four guys got out. They started pounding the shit out of the door that would have been mine if I had stayed. If I'd been there, they wouldn't have been professional.

They left. I took the money I'd brought and went to a club. The next day, I went right back home—alive and in one piece, neither of which I might have been if I'd been a little more trusting of the clientele.

24

6. Drugs Arrive

It was a couple of other incidents that convinced me to find another line of work. Once, my roommate had a warrant out for his arrest, and the cops mistakenly arrested me instead. If they'd checked around a bit, they'd have found more than enough to put me away for a while. Knowing that I'd come that close scared the shit out of me.

Then a friend of mine actually got busted, and ended up getting sentenced to a decade in the clink (I think he's out now, but we're not friends anymore). I went to see him in jail, and we talked about some friends he'd made, and some old ones he'd run back into on the inside.

Then he looked me in the eye, and got more serious than I'd ever seen him.

"Get out while you can," he warned me. "You're on TV now. You're going to lose your job. You're going to lose everything." I'd never heard him talk like that before. It wasn't that he was an uncaring person, but we didn't really interact on any kind of sympathetic level.

I heard him. I followed his advice. That day, I got out of selling drugs forever.

But not out of the drug business entirely. In a few years, I'd be back in, on the other side of the product.

7

The Call of Wrestling

Between bounty hunts, I'd somehow managed to find a way back to the gridiron. A buddy of mine had invited me to a semipro game in Forest Park, a few minutes south of Atlanta. I'd just *happened* to have a chat with the coach, who *somehow* knew that I had a past in the game. By total coincidence, I'd ended up on his team.

As the season wound down, I'd gotten friendly with a teammate named Melvin, who told me about another athletic dream of his.

"I've been training to be a wrestler," he told me, "but I can't afford it anymore. But I can train you and make you a star."

No thanks. Not just because so few guys in wrestling ever become stars, but because I just wasn't interested. Aside from seeing wrestling here and there over the years, I'd never been a fan of wrestling, and certainly didn't want to try it myself.

But he kept nagging me and, as much to shut him up as to explore a new endeavor, I gave it a shot. I learned the basics: how to take bumps (falls), roll on the mat, act like you're being hurt (called "selling," which I'd find out later), locking up, the same things everyone learns early on.

I stuck with it. I admit I liked it; it was kind of fun, doing that stuff. But how could I really know how good I was without someone with a hell of a lot more time in the business than Melvin, himself hardly even a trainer, to let me know? Then someone did.

This guy had as much the *look* of a wrestler as anyone ever had. Melvin and I kept trying to convince ourselves that we weren't intimidated by someone about twice our size put together, someone who'd been all over the world, beaten the hell out of people bigger than him (such a person was tough to imagine), and won titles up and down the East Coast and in Japan.

Even now, almost thirty years later, I'm still not sure how Ray Candy looked at me and saw a future New Jack. No idea what made him know, or even think, that I had anything near what it took to go anywhere in wrestling, even outside of some shoebox arena in Atlanta.

"Listen to me," Candy told me. "You'll go a long way in this business, but you have to trust me."

What else could I say? "Alright!"

Right around then came a moment that would change (*make* might be a better word) my wrestling career.

I was checking out the flick *New Jack City*, watching Wesley Snipes love his moneymaking, drug-selling life, and Ice T (one year before his rap song "Cop Killer" blasted a fault line through American entertainment), as a detective, trying to bring him down. Like almost always happens in these movies, the man up top shows that he's touchable after all, going down from gunfire.

Long after the film, that title phrase stuck with me. New Jack. *New Jack*. Would audiences go for that, chant-wise? Years before that, they'd rooted for Dusty Rhodes like crazy, blaring "Dust-ee! Dust-ee!" at the top of their lungs. Later on, I'd work with future music Hall of Famer Bootsy Collins on an entrance intro, one I still use today. At his concerts, even at his appearances, people still roared "Boot-see! Boot-see!" until their voice boxes quit working.

Could I get them to do that for me? A good name is integral in wrestling: "Mean Mark" Callous' career would have ended long ago if he hadn't become the Undertaker, just like Steve Austin wouldn't have gone anywhere if he'd kept that Ringmaster name the WWE first gave him. You think Hulk Hogan would have become a legend if he'd stayed the Thunderlips guy he played in *Rocky III*?

If fans can't say your name without snickering, think it's too ridiculous to chant or write about, you're not going to get anywhere, no matter how you look or what moves you can do. I needed to find something that made people know that *this* motherfucker was here to stay, and that fucking with him would end with you getting hurt. They needed to want to see me kick the shit out of people that got in my way.

New Jack. It sounded right. It sounded like a name that would get right into audiences' minds and get their attention. Maybe scare them a little. But definitely make them want to keep watching, and cheering (or booing!) and paying.

It's been working for me for almost thirty years. Talk about striking moniker gold.

Ray kept working with me, and soon I was spending my weekends performing in front of tiny crowds in Atlanta. It's amazing how many of the most memorable moments in my career have come with so few in the stands, which is why I'm glad that someone's all but guaranteed to film you and put it straight on the Internet today.

And I noticed something about those slowly increasing crowds. People came. People cheered. People booed. If a wrestler can get fans to do that sort of thing—and pay to do it!—something's going right. Just knowing that I could have that effect on so many people so early in my career, so quickly in the ring, made me feel like I'd found treasure in the most unexpected spot!

But Ray also cautioned me about something else that I was sure to encounter in wrestling. As a black man wrestling throughout the 1970s and '80s, often as the heel, he'd heard more than his share of threats and the N-word. That's an opponent that you can't pin and defeat, no matter how many weapons you have.

To that point, I'd been pretty lucky with racism, although that wouldn't last. I could remember being in third grade and being shocked at the number of white kids that were suddenly getting bused into their new school; I could remember being suddenly and very heavily outnumbered in the racial sense. My black friends and I, however few were left in class, had gotten over it, but those had been some awkward weeks.

It hit harder when I got to adulthood. One day in 1989, three white friends and myself were on a bounty hunt in Mississippi. In unfamiliar territory, we asked for breakfast recommendations from the first gas station attendant we could find around dawn.

"There's a diner downtown," he informed us. "They [my friends] can go in there, but you can't."

"Why is that?" I asked.

"Well," he said, sounding almost apologetic, "they don't allow black people to come in there."

We got there, and right away we could feel the tension thicken to iron. We walked in the place, and it seemed to go almost silent, like people couldn't believe their lying eyes.

Tough shit for them. It was a buffet, the perfect spot for four starving guys looking to carb up for an exciting day. I stepped forward and started to fill my personal tank.

Then I noticed something. A tray that had been jammed with food—food I'd sampled a moment ago—was now empty. Then another. Then another. I'd walk by, load a bit on my plate, and step away, and when I glanced back, it had all disappeared.

And then I realized why. Some asshole server was following me around, snatching up the platters I'd touched. Probably any that I'd even looked at or breathed in the direction of.

I just laughed. What else can you do? These people were wasting tons of food, and the money they'd spent on it, because they looked at a black man and saw some sort of male Typhoid Mary (Mary's brother Malachi, maybe?).

My friend noticed it, too, and he wasn't as laid back as I'd come across.

"We're going to fix these motherfuckers," he vowed to me.

He started eating off my plate, and I started eating off of his. Pretty soon, all of us were eating off each other's plates. We might have looked crazy to some people, but we were a hell of a lot less ignorant than our neighbors were acting at the time.

We'd look around, and almost feel the rays coming at us from furious eyes everywhere. But there were fewer and fewer—not because people just gave up and got used to it, but because many actually started to get up and leave.

Again, it was hurting these bigots more than it was hurting me. These people had just paid for a meal they found a sad reason not to enjoy. I bet many of them didn't come back to the place, not after seeing one of *us* there!

We paid—but we *didn't* leave a tip! The ultimate "fuck you" to the service industry.

I remember thinking it was nuts that it was 1989 and people were still thinking like that. Sadly, I'd see many more such examples at later dates.

But right then, I was worrying more and more about wrestling. I don't spend time with regret, so I didn't really start wishing I'd done it sooner or anything, but I was glad I was doing it now. I was good at this! Pretty soon, I was about the hottest, if not the most talented, that small federation had ever seen.

Melvin was getting ticked that things were happening faster for his trainee (or former trainee) than for him.

"I'm going to stick with wrestling," I told him, "but I want to be on TV." Even back then, I knew how important the square box in the living room was for success in the squared circle.

"Man, that's going to take some time," he cautioned.

"Maybe for you," I responded, "but I'm going to be on TV." I wasn't going to wait around—then as now, no one gives you anything in your wrestling career. You've got to go out and get it yourself.

Melvin didn't; he quit pretty soon after that. But I had heard of a promoter nearby named Sammy Kent who ran the North Georgia Wrestling Alliance. Once again, with luck and go-getterness on my side, I put together a tape of my earliest work and landed a meeting with him. A few days later, he called me back, and I went straight to work with him.

That particular alliance, however, wouldn't last long because someone else came calling—someone well known to just about any longtime fans of wrestling.

And they always will for me—just not for the best of reasons.

8

Crossing to the USWA

The voice boomed over the telephone.

"What do you guys call each other in the hood?" he asked.

I had to fight off a snicker on the other side. I loved how he was calling us "you guys." It was great the way he just assumed that I—you know, as a *brother*—was so acquainted with "hood talk." That was just wonderful.

But that might have been just the kind of person Jerry Jarrett was. He'd been around the business since I was in kindergarten, so maybe this was just how you get started in wrestling. Sometimes you have to do some tongue-biting for the greater good to get anywhere in the squared circle. I was the newbie and he was the veteran, so now I was going to clamp my mouth shut just long enough to swallow my pride, and maybe get a shot in his United States Wrestling Association.

"Well, lots of things," I answered. "Sometimes we call each other homies, homeboys...."

"That's it!" he jumped. "We're going to call him Homeboy!"

Not me. I was already New Jack, and I was never going to change. Jarrett wanted me to debut alongside one of the few other black men in the area, but he couldn't think of a way to tie us together with a more common thread than just skin tone. I'd barely gotten a foothold in the company in a few singles matches in mid–1992, and he figured I could learn from sharing the ring with some more experienced folk.

I wasn't sure my new friend Mark Frear would go for it. He'd been bouncing around wrestling—a hell of a lot more territorial in those days—showing up in the WWF and all over the East Coast before landing in the USWA just after I did, and I didn't know if he'd want to share the spotlight at all, especially with a guy with much less experience than him. That, and to change his gimmick to go along with mine, I was asking quite a bit. Jarrett didn't want to ask Mark himself, maybe because he wanted me to get blamed if things went the wrong way.

They almost did, and very fast.

I called Mark and told him about being Homeboy. He fucking lost it. Yelling, screaming, cussing at me, freaking out. He was from Baltimore, he was smart, educated, well spoken, as far from a "street kid" as one could get (not that I was of the sort myself). He bitched and moaned and groused about how it wasn't going to work, how he wasn't going to do it, and everything else.

Then he agreed. Like I said, it's just how so many young wrestlers start. Even after a few years in the business, he was pretty much a glorified rookie, a newcomer still trying to "get over" with fans and promoters.

Anyway, we started teaming up in full-blown street garb. I didn't really care how I looked just yet; I was just trying to learn more about the trade. But I saw Mark with a gold chain around his neck and huge MC Hammer–type pants, and I almost held up our first entrance from laughing so hard. Believe me, anyone who saw me doing this character today (and I'm sure there are probably some clips hidden on a secret website somewhere) would never in a million years believe this is the guy who ended up as New Jack!

But Jarrett must have liked it. The fans sure as hell must have. Because it didn't take us long to grab the first title of my short career, taking home the USWA tag title in June 1993.

Before we even got the chance to take another sip from the cup of championship coffee, however, the belts were off our waists less than three weeks later. That sort of had to happen, although Jarrett, myself, and a very few others were the only ones who knew why.

From the moment I'd arrived in the USWA, they had told me that I was only going to be there six weeks. I ended up staying a little longer than that, but I knew I'd be in and out. That's why I didn't really establish a foundation in the Memphis area.

The same, unfortunately, can't be said for Mark. Expecting a long stay in the USWA, if not a place at the federation's top, he'd actually moved to Nashville with his girlfriend. When he found out I was only going to be there a short while, he went back out of his fucking mind.

Sadly, back in 2014, I got a phone call saying that Mark had died. He'd stayed close to Baltimore after the USWA, quitting the business in the late 1990s. I never got the whole story as to how he passed, and I couldn't find it as I was putting this book together.

I didn't exactly feel great about leaving, but I wasn't worried. It's part of the business. You go somewhere, get an opportunity to meet some people, hopefully do some business, then go off somewhere else. You keep meeting people, keep making good impressions on the promoters and the fans until your name gets big enough for someone to call you a long-term investment. In a world before people could rely on the Internet to know everything, you had to do most of the work yourself.

After spending so much of my youth just waiting to move to the next spot, I was ready for my adulthood to be about the same. I'd gotten started in Georgia, so there's no reason I couldn't continue back there.

Because I had a few other, rougher reasons to believe I'd never make it in the USWA.

Once of which I sort of brought on myself. Young whiz kid that I was, I got a custom-made license plate for my new Fiero reading "New Jack: Pro Wrestler." Yeah, I just *had* to let everyone know who I was and what I did.

From the start, guys in the dressing room were asking if they could have their picture taken with my car. Every week, a new guy, or guys, would be posing with my wheels, pointing at the license plate, laughing. I thought they really liked it, that they thought it was a cool car. It wasn't until later—too late—that I realized that they were making fun of me. Busting the chops of the new kid who wanted everyone to think he was so great, mocking his license plate. They were showing those pictures to their friends, letting everyone know about this newbie. Those guys were laughing at me over that for years.

My other reason, though, was quite a bit sadder.

Although he'd actually been the one to invite me to the USWA, Jerry Lawler and I had never gotten along. One night, he and Jarrett had been sitting together at the Mid-South Coliseum in Memphis. Two women were in the ring having it out, knowing that whoever lost would be getting launched into a bucket of mud. One of them was Miss Texas. A few years later, she'd be known to WWF fans as Jacqueline. On March 14, 2016, she became the first black woman inducted into the WWE Hall of Fame.

That night, she ended up getting thrown into the mud. Lawler and Jarrett were watching the match. Unbeknownst to them, I was standing right behind them. I had to ask someone something, but I wasn't going to interrupt.

Lawler glanced at Jarrett. "Look at the little wet nigger dog!" said the King.

I couldn't believe it. I couldn't even move, talk, react at all. Then Lawler noticed me.

"Oh, hey, New Jack," he said. "What can I do for you?" Not a fucking thing. Everything I wanted to ask him went right out of my mind. I turned around and walked away. A few weeks later, I was gone.

Jarrett and I were OK. I told him I was leaving. He thanked me for coming up, and said he hoped we could work together again soon. I wasn't sure if he said that to everyone, but I hoped I'd done what a newcomer should do as I headed back south.

My issues with Lawler never went away. They actually got worse. In the summer of 2018, they blew up all over the country.

I hadn't thought much of his son Brian either. He always came across to me, and to a *lot* of others, like, just since he'd been sired by the King, his self-proclaimed loyalty gave him the right to look down on us. He never had to worry about looking good for the higher-ups in the business and making first impressions, because he'd always have the family name to use as leverage. He knew that, and he enjoyed reminding us of that.

But I felt he was just a jerk. You find those in almost every locker room. His dad had bigger issues that someone should have called him on long ago. But he's the King, he's the guy that *made* wrestling in Tennessee. He's so fucking special that everyone tried so hard to ignore it.

But not me. After his son killed himself in July 2018, I went on Twitter mocking both of them, saying it should have been Daddy right there with him. Did people think I was just saying that to get attention, or because I've just got a chunk of ice in my chest? No fucking way. I had every right and reason to wish bad on him. Still do.

Yeah, I knew some people were going to be pissed about that. But New Jack has never held his tongue, in or out of character, before, so what did anyone expect? And I know, still know to this day, that I was saying things that most other people were thinking, and had been thinking for a long time. That's why all the self-righteous hypocrites who blasted me for saying that didn't bother me.

Oh, the guy was suffering? Big fucking deal. That didn't erase all the wrong he'd done. I was supposed to forget all the shit I had with this guy? Not me. Some grudges are worth holding on to, and I'm a pretty good grudge carrier.

I got thrown off of Twitter. I didn't give a fuck. I didn't need it before and don't need it now. You're not going to get me to say I was wrong.

Anyway, after six action-packed USWA weeks, I headed back to the Peach State. I wouldn't be there long, but the next phase of my career would lead me to fame.

9

Back to Georgia

My reasons for coming back to Georgia were pretty simple. It wasn't about sentiment—you can guess that that's never been a part of my personality. It wasn't even for the money, although I wouldn't ever be working for free. The stable work was nice, working with people I knew I'd already impressed in front of fans who appreciated me, but that wasn't all of it.

I can tell you in less than one word—television. More of it than I ever would have gotten in the USWA.

I didn't give a shit if it was 24 hours a day, if it was on every night, or if it was before dawn on a Saturday (guess which one it ended up being?). For one of the first times in my career, people could see New Jack without buying a ticket. It's as close as wrestlers get to free advertising.

Soon after I got back to the Alliance, Sammy and the rest up top showed how much they trusted me, handing me the first world title belt of my career. Of course, I'll never forget that, but it really wasn't what I'd call a career highlight. There are many more parts of my career, many that you'll read about very soon, that had nothing to do with a title and still meant more to me.

Does that sound strange? Most people would probably have a tough time believing it. You'd think that most wrestlers would remember their first title like it was yesterday. But not me, and I think that's been a benefit to my career over the long term. I never got caught up in political bullshit in wrestling, fighting over a belt, winning it, losing it. A belt's nice, but if you need one to complete your persona, you're putting yourself at a disadvantage. There are too many guys who need to be the champion as part of their ring persona, people who are nothing if they're not at the top. Many people outside of wrestling think that a belt's something to judge wrestlers on, like one guy's better than another because the first guy was the champ for longer than the second, or had more reigns.

That's not how I feel, never have. I never needed to be the champion to be the best.

So it didn't bother me when I lost the belt pretty soon after I got it. I was getting paid the same amount and getting the same TV time whether or not I was the champ. But that's about the time I started working with a guy that I'd come to know as my tag partner for a long time.

The wrestling world would know him as Mustafa Saed.

I was up to no good in North Georgia, just like Jack. He was selling drugs and wrestling, and I was doing the same thing. I was bigger than him, and he had a bigger mouth—he could speak better than anyone I've ever heard.—Mustafa Saed

---

I'd been working with Mustafa for a while, and he'd been doing all kind of crazy shit, eating raw meat with his face painted, playing a sheik. He was in WCW doing jobs on Saturday mornings.

"Bro, that ain't where you need to be!" I told him one day (he was one of the few people I spoke to, another tradition I'd follow through my career). "Want to be my partner?"

"Jack," he responded, "I was going to ask you the same thing!"

We started teaming up, and it didn't take long before we got in front of the right pair of eyes, two that hid behind some legendary glasses.

Sammy got a call from a guy named Jim Cornette, who'd been one of the most visible faces and most-heard voices in wrestling for some time, although I wasn't highly acquainted with his work at that point. A few years ago, he'd started Smoky Mountain Wrestling in Tennessee, and stretched it down through the Carolinas and to Georgia. Now he was visiting the Cobb County Civic Center in Marietta, and hoped Mustafa and I could and would do our thing for a larger crowd and for him. The guy always had a great eye for talent, which he'd prove later while helping to find some for both the WWE and TNA.

Now he just might want us.

You hear about movie stars performing on street corners before they make it big. I'm a big Clint Eastwood fan, and he used to get beat up first, and then make a great comeback for people for coins. That's how we were in Georgia. It was a stepping-stone for the next level.—Mustafa Saed

---

Whatever we did that night, it worked. He saw something in us that made him offer us a Smoky shot.

9. Back to Georgia

Right around that time, though, I suffered one of the most personal losses of my career, though far from the last.

I still called Ray all the time, as he was still training people back in Georgia. He always told me, "Jack, don't let these white people make a flunky out of you. Stick to your guns. Stay true to what you know, but don't let them make a flunky out of you." He told me I could always call him, and I always did, and he always talked to me. I could be riding back home at 2 a.m., and if I had something to call him about, he'd talk to me.

I knew his health hadn't been great; I don't think anyone who weighs about 350 pounds is in perfect shape. I'd seen him the weekend before coming from a show and talked to him on a Thursday.

When I got home that Sunday, a buddy of mine called. He told me that Ray Candy had died. Just forty-two, my first wrestling mentor's heart had given out for the last time.

10

Climbing the Mountain

> *When the Gangstas got to Smoky Mountain Wrestling, they drove in a nice Corvette. I told them, "Park that Corvette and buy a $300 car, because when people see you with your car, they're going to tear it to pieces!" They bought an old van with the wheels on one side bigger than the other, but it kept them alive.* — *WWE Hall of Famer Ricky Morton*

For one brief moment, two groups whose ideas couldn't possibly be farther apart found a common ground. Maybe a common enemy would be a better way to say it.

And who cared if it had to be over pro wrestling, and if the villain in question had to be me? That's just the price I paid for uniting the NAACP and the Ku Klux Klan, right in the middle of an area where people *still* do too much skin-color judging.

Even being champions down in Georgia hadn't been enough for Mustafa and I; millions of people had heard Jim Cornette's microphone motormouth for years with all those guys in the Midnight Express and everywhere else, but it only took one tryout tag match in Atlanta to get him on the phone with us. He'd started Smoky Mountain Wrestling in 1991, and now he wanted a few new someones.

Despite the match being on in the early morning hours, Cornette had caught it. Then he'd rang up on the other side of Sammy Kent's phone, and eventually mine. He told me he wanted a black tag team that would A. be heels, and B. work well with a microphone in our faces. Personally, I thought a couple of black men beating the shit out of some white guys in Virginia, West Virginia, Tennessee, and everywhere around there wouldn't need to talk at all to be hated, but he said that was wrong.

"I want you to be racist," he said. "Anything you can say that's racist, put it in a promo and say it."

> *The promo and the look that New Jack had when I saw him on that show, in the back of my mind, I thought, "My God, this guy's got a lot of presence." He could cut a promo where you believed that he believed what he was saying. That's the whole secret to wrestling: not what you say, but whether other people believe it.—Jim Cornette*

He wanted us to be the Gangsters. I agreed, but we needed a slight phonetic switch. When you look at the movies about gangs, or when you're in a gang in the hood, it's *gangstas*! It's how we say it, how we yell it, how we proclaim how proud we are of our street ranks.

Wrestling in SMW's stomping grounds (pun intended!) of not just Tennessee, but Kentucky, North Carolina, and Virginia, a couple of scary black men weren't going to be universally beloved to begin with, so why not start at the other end, and then expand the breaking point?

We were off to a great start with the name, and Cornette was the perfect guy to help us reach the high level of hatred, to give audiences a reason to *really* dislike us as people, for reasons far worse—and, sadly, legitimate!—than the color of our skin.

New Jack and Mustafa would proudly explain to everyone that would listen that we were from the slums of South Central Los Angeles, and ready to take everything we'd learned there and do some serious showing and telling.

> *On the cartoons, they always have the big guy looking like the dumb-dumb, and the little guy's the tougher, smarter guy. When we were presented like that, it looked like that to other people. I didn't care, as long as we made money.— Mustafa Saed*

This was early 1994, so everyone was way too familiar with the Rodney King riots that had knocked race relations back a bit and hurt a ton of people and businesses. And us black men got our own special sort of revenge for that one night at a high school show in Virginia. Mustafa and I and everyone suddenly pulled out nightsticks and blackjacks and beat down Ricky Morton in the middle of the ring! The King beat-down with the races reversed!

> *Everybody had accused us of being too far behind the times*
> *for doing "old-fashioned wrestling the way you like it!" Well,*
> *I gave people a gimmick that said, "This is on the news*
> *every night right now!" They didn't sound like they were*
> *from L.A., but I don't think people gave a shit. We were in*
> *Kentucky once, and the ring announcer said they were from*
> *"south central Louisiana!"—Jim Cornette*

The next year, after the King beating and riots, another tragedy had occurred in that neck of the woods, one that would, throughout 1995 and 1996, spark racism even more, cutting wounds that many feel are still around today. Now we'd use it to go deeper than any wrestling promotion had ever had the balls to go before.

"Cut a promo to make white people mad," Cornette advised. "Say whatever you can think of that's going to piss white people off."

"Jim," I said, "that's fine. But I'm a heel, we're the bad guys, and I don't just want to make white people mad; I want to make *everybody* mad." I asked him what he wanted, and he said it didn't really matter, just to think of something. I don't think even he expected me to go where I'd end up.

Mustafa and I whaled hell out of a pair of jobbers—the term for wrestlers routinely defeated by champions and up-and-comers. No way were two white boys going to get anything off the new guys. We were there to take revenge for centuries of hate and violence against our brothers and sisters, and these two would be the first to pay the price.

A beat-down SMW fans had hardly seen before, and then a three-count that showed that they'd never had a chance. SMW was *lucky* that we'd stopped by to show them how to work. Not like we wanted to be there.

Then we stepped up to cut the promo that blasted far out of SMW territory.

> *I thought several times he was going to have a hemorrhage*
> *or stroke! In those hot high school gyms, he'd have a match,*
> *and then go and talk for two and a half minutes at the*
> *top of his lungs. I couldn't do that! I told Jack to make his*
> *promos real. They were not playing to a sympathetic part of*
> *the country; people in that part weren't high on civil rights*
> *injustice.—Jim Cornette*

Like Cornette, interviewer Bob Caudle was from wrestling's old school, where traditionalism ruled the show. We were as far from tradition as wrestling could get. I'd put all kinds of time and thought into this rage-fest. I was going to make history, but not like most people hope for.

Even in character, Bob looked off-balance as he held a microphone in my face. Even after the two decades he'd spent in wrestling, I don't think it was all an act. I was about to take the present and ram it straight down everyone's windpipe.

"Thirty years ago, we'd have been strung up in somebody's tree," I roared, "getting hung for beating up two white boys!" If I'd stopped right there, half the crowd would have acted out my words if they could get their hands on me. But I wasn't anywhere near done.

"I don't like being up here!" I continued. "I was getting out of a car, I slipped and fell, and it was in tobacco spit. There ain't nothing but rednecks up here! Nothing but coal miners, chicken farmers, Klansmen!" Now the rest of the arena was pissed at me. Even some of my fellow wrestlers were probably upset. Caudle looked like a blind man in a maze.

"Violence to you," I told the crowd, "might be putting somebody in a figure four. Violence to me is taking a can of gas, pouring it on you, and setting you on fire. I didn't come up here to be liked!" Talk about stating the obvious.

Then I went for it all. I decided to hit the crowd, and the white race of America, exactly where it was just starting to hurt, and would keep hurting for a very long time.

"I'd like to send a special shout out to my homeboy O. J. Simpson," I asserted. "Keep up the good work! Two less to worry about!"

If there's been a promo in the history of wrestling that pissed people off more, that made things that personal, I've never heard it. The audience wanted me dead—those in the arena who heard my words firsthand, and those watching me on TV. People in the audience were screaming at the top of their lungs, calling me every name in the book and some that weren't even in the book. Caudle looked dumbfounded, like even he couldn't believe I'd exploded like that.

It didn't stop there. Newspapers have never been too big on covering pro wrestling, probably afraid they'd make it sound legitimate, but my words were mentioned in pages far outside the SMW territory. TV stations kicked us off the air. People blasted the shit out of me, Cornette, everyone. If the Internet had been around then, there's no telling what would have happened. It's been almost a quarter-century since I blasted out those words, and even today, people still bring it up when I'm signing autographs at a show. They probably always will.

New Jack

On the mic, I don't think even the Rock would have a chance against New Jack! I didn't need to say anything. All I did was make gestures showing that I agreed with him.—Mustafa Saed

SMW learned its lesson: from then on, every time the Gangstas showed up on television, they'd put a disclaimer on the show, warning people that what I would say would probably offend somebody. That covered their asses and mine; it allowed me to get away with it and no one could complain.

But in wrestling, any publicity is great, whether it's the media, the fans, whoever. If your name gets out and into enough mouths and minds, you're going to go somewhere.

In our case, we really *needed* bad publicity. We wanted everybody to be mad at us. We had to be hated, by everyone. Not just the white people, who threw things at us, spit at us, called us niggers all the time, but everyone, even our black brothers and sisters. If we just badmouthed white people, the black communities might have gotten behind us, gotten all radicalized, and even agreed with how ticked we sounded, and that could have caused some problems.

So I even turned up the intra-racial heat. I badmouthed Martin Luther King, Jr., because, unlike him, the Gangstas hit back so much harder than they were struck. I reminded my mostly white audience that they didn't really like King, only pretended to after he got killed, so I didn't like him either. I told everyone how even Medger Evers wasn't my role model. We ate fried chicken and watermelon in the ring, and rubbed Affirmative Action in everyone's face. I reminded my "brothers and sisters" how many of them were on welfare. I told the NAACP to kiss my black ass! I called them sellouts, homegrown monkeys, everything. I just went off on everybody.

Hey, wouldn't it be interesting to see if I could get over like that today, if I were praising Trump? I'd go out to the ring with one of his red hats with that "Make America Great Again" stuff on it, maybe even waving an American flag and carrying a huge poster of him or something. I'd be yelling shit at the crowd like, "You're one of those sorry niggers on welfare! No more free daycare or food stamps! We're going to cut out all that 'baby mama' shit right now!" A black man spewing that at high volume in the south might get over like crazy with certain people and hated like hell by others. If I wandered into the WWE stomping grounds of New York—Hillary Clinton country—with that, I'd probably get shot.

10. Climbing the Mountain

I told New Jack once, "You could take your talent, go to a nightclub, and be the DJ that walks around and raps to everybody in the club!" He could take that microphone in the ring, and he was funny, with a great sense of humor. People just ate him up.—Tod Gordon

I'm the first to admit that it's my mouth as much as my moves that got me over—and kept me there—in the ring, and has been since I told the cold hard truth to the fans way back in Smoky Mountain. Put me in front of a microphone, and I'm truly New Jack. I don't even remember Jerome at all when I'm trying to talk up a match and draw people into a building.

Sometimes being great on a microphone can cause people, though usually only for a short while, to forget, or at least look past, a performer's lack of ability in the ring.

For my entire career, people came up to me all the time trying to figure out how my promo skills got so sharp. That's not bragging; you'll hear throughout this book from those who believed I had some kind of mic-rolling sixth sense. What was my secret?

My answer was simple: nothing.

There was no great secret to cutting a strong promo, just like there was no easy way to suddenly morph into some chatterbox champion. I just took the mic and spoke from my dark, angry heart. It was all always right off the top of my head.

But it wasn't easy. When my mic skills first got tried out way back in Georgia, I was the most camera-shy motherfucker in Sammy Kent's land down south. I couldn't make lens-to-lens combat with a filmer, so I hid. During my promos, a large pair of sunglasses concealed that my eyes weren't even open.

Slowly, I got better at it. I attempted to cut a promo pretending I was talking to someone on the street. I was looking straight at the camera now, but it wasn't the camera anymore; it was someone who needed a point made clear by any verbal means necessary. I got really good at doing promos in one take.

Just as Paul Heyman would very soon, Cornette learned quickly how much of an asset my promo chops could be. He'd just tell me a few points to touch on, and to do the best I can.

So often, people came to me for help with this, and almost always left disappointed. I just tried to explain that I didn't have any hidden power

43

or know much more than they did when it came to wrestling. I'd see guys writing their promos, recording them, listening to themselves chat.

> *New Jack could get a crowd going in two seconds. He helped me a lot when I was on the microphone, because I'd never done that before. He told me, "Look, you can talk, but there's other things you should consider, like the rhythm of how you speak, how you stand, how you feed off the crowd." I was very mechanical, and it helped me become more animated.—Lou "Sign Guy Dudley" D'Angeli*

Of course I can't badmouth them for that. If it worked for them—and it did for some, who turned into great talkers—I was fine with it. I told them to make eye contact with the lens and talk to someone who they'd just met on the street.

For some it worked. For others, not so much. Some people might have thought that my drug use helped my promo work, but I never thought of it that way. Like I said, I'm not necessarily special in that I can do these pretty fast just from pulling them off the top of my bald, scarred head. It's just a question that can have different and all correct answers for all wrestlers.

> *There was still enough believability (in wrestling) in the south at the time that the NAACP went to Sandy Scott, the public "owner," even though Jim Cornette was the commissioner. Cornette was a heel at the time, so they couldn't go to him! We ended up telling them that Jack was a contractor and that he had freedom of speech, so we couldn't censor him. They said that if we let him go and he sued, they'd come in on our behalf and help us financially! We said that we couldn't do that; we had to let him have his voice!—Bill Behrens (SMW TV syndicator, later New Jack's agent)*

Public Enemy blared out "Shut 'Em Down" and "Can't Truss It" as we rolled to the ring (Cornette says it's the only time he allowed rap music at his shows—a hater of rap, he'd had preferred Earth, Wind, and Fire!). I used some lines from "Fear of a Black Planet" in my promo:

> Black man, black woman, black baby,
> White man, white woman, white baby.

10. Climbing the Mountain

White man, black woman, black baby!
Black man, white woman, black baby!

The crowds went to the edge, and some went flying right over. We'd be walking out to the ring, and rednecks would be leaning over the balconies to spit on us, and there were some weird combos there: saliva, tobacco, food, all kinds of shit. It got to where security would be walking us out with a tarp over us. If we'd have been lynched in the middle of the ring, everyone might have cheered on the hangmen.

Yeah, Cornette loved it, but he was in the extreme minority. Whites, blacks, everyone hated us. That's not the point. In wrestling, people can love you, hate you—as long as they're feeling something strong enough about you to buy a ticket or turn on their TV to see you, it doesn't hardly matter at all. Even the SMW crew team teamed up against us, putting aside the whole heel/face labels to fight the greater bad.

In the big towns, it did well, but in the small towns, truthfully, the Gangstas did not get over. Instead of "We want to see people beat their ass!" heat, it was more, "We don't want to be in the same building with these motherfuckers!" heat! I underestimated the level of racism that still existed. The Gangstas were cutting-edge, but they were too far ahead for Eastern Kentucky.—Jim Cornette

---

All that, though, was just for the cameras. Away from the ring, we were all acting out *Animal House*–type shit.

We lived in Atlanta, so they had to fly us up every week for a show. That's when the parties began.

Cornette had a townhouse that he was renting for all the boys who stayed out of town. We'd show up at the townhouse on Thursday, stay for the weekend and do shows, and then head out on Sunday.

If we weren't too hung-over or stoned to shit, me, Mustafa, Bruiser Bedlam, Balls Mahoney, Glen Jacobs (yeah, you know, the guy who ended up as Kane in the WWE, and then as mayor of a town in Tennessee! Wonder if he'd let the Gangstas do their thing there now?) and some others had all kinds of shit going on in that house. We'd get drunk, have parties, invite people to come out and hang out with us, generally just acting like damn fools.

And things got scary sometimes. I had a green Corvette with a Malcolm X license plate on it, and the cops knew it was mine, and where we lived. One night, Balls borrowed my car to go to the store.

Thinking it was me, the cops followed him, and pulled him over. Then they pulled him out of the car at gunpoint.

"Where is New Jack?" they demanded, ready to re-enact the King beating. "This is his car, so why are you driving it?" He thought they were going to arrest him, or maybe even use their guns or nightsticks, but they finally let him go.

The promos were just one more brick to the wall of us being hated, and we were. Always with the nigger shit, threatened lynchings, the whole nine. But people kept coming from all over, hoping to get us destroyed. Didn't happen. We won match after match.

But not by fighting fair. No great heel ever has.

We'd had backups since our time in Georgia, teams of large black men that would scare the Fruit of Islam escorting us to the ring and back, making damn sure we never got a taste of our own medicine. When we came to SMW, Cornette wanted to find some black guys to walk us to the ring.

In Knoxville, that was easy, because there were lots of black people. But when we went to West Virginia or Kentucky or Virginia, I didn't see many hanging around.

Then I saw a guy named Accie Connor doing a tryout match on TV. He'd been working with the big guys in the WWF, and he looked like he knew what he was doing in there.

I called Cornette, and he liked the man, too. We'd found the Gangstas' new bodyguard—and his new name was D'Lo Brown. Like us, he'd someday move into wrestling's big leagues.

10. Climbing the Mountain

Our next opponents had been to the top and would get back. They're still doing it today.

After kicking the shit out of almost everybody who dared to even make eye contact with a Gangsta for a while, we went into a program with the Rock 'n' Roll Express, *the* team in that area. I hadn't been in the business long at all, and now we were working with Ricky Morton and Robert Gibson.

And, hey, why not? Maybe we could do them the type of damage that a few different versions of Cornette's Midnight Express couldn't.

We'd worked with the Harris Brothers and the Heavenly Bodies, but the Gangstas were something new, and it's great any time you have someone new like that in our business. People knew New Jack was good with a microphone. New Jack and Mustafa listened to us. They learned about the heat—how to get it and how to keep it. I never had to worry about getting hurt.—Ricky Morton

---

But with all our tricks, heat, foreign objects, whatever, we couldn't get the titles off them. So we did something that had hardly been seen in wrestling before. With all the traditionalism of SMW, this would break some serious ground.

Long before those backstage skits were common in WCW or the WWF, Cornette put together a vignette where we stood before a judge, pleading our case that the bigotry I'd bugled about on microphones for so long was the reason we weren't wearing SMW gold. The Midnight Express may have beaten us, but only because they, like every other white man at the time (or so New Jack would tell anyone listening!), were doing everything in their power to take down the brothers!

It worked. He ruled in our favor. The Gangstas had become champions without even entering an arena!

Things kept taking off. We took the audience back to where the Gangstas originated, doing a video from the streets of South Central (actually, it was a little project in Atlanta called Beaumont Homes).

I talked about how all that mattered here was how good you looked, how much money you had, how many women you could rack up, how the black man was finally getting revenge for everything that had been done to him for too long.

Brothers from all over town came to cheer, to high-five their Gangsta friends, to join in the revolution we'd made happen in the squared circle. For the first time, the Gangstas had some fans.

No one knew that they'd just been a bunch of guys who happened to be sitting around the area, and that I'd just gone around asking them if they'd like to be in the video.

With that video, the impossible unity began. The NAACP started picketing us in Atlanta, letting everyone know that we didn't represent our race. Farther north, the Ku Klux Klan came around, for reasons pretty obvious, and with a message not so far from the NAACP's. We'd taken two eternal enemies and brought them together—against us.

But it was for us as well as for SMW. You see, even when they were picketing, they were buying tickets to do it. They could sit in the front row like they were back in the 60s doing a lunch counter sit-in, cheering, booing, or whatever else, but we didn't give a fuck. If they paid to see us, they could do, or not do, whatever they wanted!

The heat was legit. You could feel it, make it tangible. These people wanted us dead. It was scary, going to little towns in Kentucky and not know what was waiting for you. There were times when Jimmy said to get in our cars and drive back to Knoxville. Not to stop for gas, for food, for nothing. You could look and see the hate in some people's eyes.—D'Lo Brown

---

What else could we do? Quite a bit, as it turned out. We were still drawing, still making money against the Express, and then going to the mat with Tracy Smothers and, not quite so ironically, Tony Anthony, monikered the Dirty White Boy. That's when we started doing the hardcore/ street fight-type brawling that would get us noticed soon by a different "ring leader."

When you're the heel, it ain't what you do; it's how you do it. The babyface you're selling for, you don't have to hit him eighty-five times. You just hit him one time and he sells it. I had to make New Jack understand what our business is all about. When you learn that magic, it's the best thing in the world. I had to help him understand how to make things mean stuff.—Ricky Morton

---

And if we thought people were pissed at us before, there were times when we were lucky to get out of the arena alive. But sometimes I got some sad reminders that my rants against racism still had some justification.

Heading out of the ring one night, a white dude called me a nigger.

"I fucked your mama!" I snorted back. Some cops nearby heard me. When I got into the dressing room, they put me in handcuffs, and said *I* was under arrest for abusive language. Me! This asshole using that slur on a black man was perfectly OK with them, but me firing back about his mother was abusive.

They put me in jail, and I had to post bail, go to court, and pay a fine. Just for saying something in character as a wrestler. If I'd been white, they'd have given me a high-five and asked me to take a picture with their kids.

Another time, a cop showed me a newspaper article that said that a new kind of beer called Crazy Horse was making black and Hispanic drinkers go nuts. Not surprising, considering it was named after the guy that kicked Custer's ass at Little Big Horn.

I grabbed a forty-ounce of the booze and strolled out to the ring, making sure everyone there could see me guzzling away. Maybe that was the secret of my supposed insanity all along.

And again, when I came to the dressing room, the cops arrested me for drinking alcohol in public. Back to jail. Again, something that never would have happened to Cornette, Ricky, Balls, or any other man with a different shade of skin.

But it was another time, early on in my time at SMW, that I almost learned everything the hardest way.

In the midst of a battle with the Rock 'n' Rollers, a guy in the audience kept calling me nigger. Over and over again, I heard the word getting screamed at me. And whether I'm Jerome or New Jack, I'm only human, and no one can hear that bullshit for too long without losing it.

I almost did, and he almost lost everything. When the match was over, I chased the guy out of the building, into the parking lot, down the street. Mustafa was right behind me, and Ricky and Robert had my back.

Back in the dressing room, I told Ricky what had happened.

"Jack, your *point* is to piss them off!" he explained. "If you're pissing them off to the point that they're calling you that, you're doing your job!" He taught me a lot in a short time.

New Jack

New Jack almost beat the shit out of the guy. I told him, "New Jack, you need to know—we're in entertainment." He wasn't used to that. The guy wasn't going to say, "Hey, Mr. Black Man, quit beating up on Ricky Morton!"—Ricky Morton

Come to remember it, the interracial unity might not have been my top enemy-conversion accomplishment. Eventually, Cornette realized he couldn't control the monsters he'd brought in. Without any Midnight Express to bring in to battle us, he had to side with a group he'd spent years trying to destroy. The Rock 'n' Roll Express couldn't beat us on their own, so they, and he, put their differences aside in the spirit of Christmas. With him in their corner, they finally took the titles off us during the 1994 holiday season.

But we hadn't kept quiet to that point; why ruin a good habit now? I went right back to the mic, yelling and screaming about how all these evil white men had screwed us once again! Cornette had won the battle, but the war was still raging.

So he had to up the artillery. Bring in a weapon who'd taken down about everyone he'd ever faced, and was just a few years into his WWF dominance.

It was the Undertaker. The guy had terrified fans and opponents alike since he'd shown up in the WWF in late 1990.

Fear? Shit, that was a foreign word to the Gangstas. And we were going to prove it, leading the SMW fans into another vignette—this one in a graveyard, in black and white.

"If I seem kind of nervous, I'm not!" I assured the audience, and myself, as my friends wobbled in the background. "Now I'm gonna show you that the Gangstas ain't scared. I don't like being out here, but we're going to get rid of the Undertaker!"

Then a howl echoed behind us. D'Lo lost his shit, pointing and wailing. He ran off. Moments later, with "Don't Fear the Reaper" starting to creep in and a black cat sneaking out from behind a bush, we all followed in every direction.

The Dead Man arrived, and even with all our tricks and weapons, he and Smothers gave us a beating we weren't used to. By then, however, we'd already caught some other pairs of eyes.

As the Gangstas' contract was winding down in May of 1995, Al Snow came up to me one day in Johnson City, Tennessee, and told me about a company he'd worked part-time for in Philadelphia.

"Your style fits with them perfectly," he informed me. These people took everything that wrestling had done before, all the pain, risks, blood, guts, injuries, and everything else, combined it all together, and then took it up a notch. More than a few notches.

It was called Extreme Championship Wrestling for a reason.

I saw that New Jack was very charismatic—he was very talented on the mic, and he could talk people into the building. My run in Smoky Mountain was coming to an end, and Jack's was too, so I told him, "Why don't you give Paul Heyman a call? You'd have a great run there!"—Al Snow

---

I'd never heard of it, but Al was sure it would work. He'd seen us Gangstas take the street fights to people in SMW, and he knew we could do it there. We wouldn't have to change a thing.

He told me about another two guys I'd never heard of. Tod Gordon ran the joint, and Paul Heyman did the creativity. I called Tod up.

"We would love to have you here," he said, "but we want you up here in two weeks."

That was a problem. Cornette had us on the schedule for at least three more.

"ECW's offering us a deal," I told him. "I don't know how long they're having us up there, but they need us in two weeks." The feud that he and Heyman ended up taking far from professional to personal was just starting, and at this point I was stuck in the middle.

I wasn't having it. Cornette got pretty pissed, but I didn't care. It was time. We'd put in our time, given our effort and our bodies, all we could. Our contract was almost over, and we weren't winning anymore anyway, so who gave a shit?

Up to Philadelphia. And off to ECW.

11

A Taste of Extreme

New Jack had an attitude, but that was cool with me, because I had an attitude there too. I wasn't super-famous at this point.—Sandman

We'd be making our ECW premiere that very night, and we hadn't met a single person. Not tonight's opponents, not any of our co-workers, not even the people who'd assured us (over the phones) we'd be treated and paid right. Until we had that, we weren't getting anywhere near the ring.

Mustafa and I stepped through the front door at the hotel, ready for anything. We always prided ourselves on being easy to do business with, but we wanted everyone's names on all the right dotted lines. Wrestling's a business, after all, and wrestlers don't have a union to fall back on. We're all independent contractors looking for a strong deal.

He'd end up being one of our best friends in the business, but we didn't trust the Sandman when he was the first ECW person we ran into. Everyone's guards up, we met him, cautiously shook his hand, asked him where Paul and Gordon were, and moved toward Tod (Heyman was elsewhere, or so we heard).

I was Tod Gordon's boy, making sure that the guys got to the building. The only reason I was down there was to meet those dudes, to make sure they got to the arena. They got out of the fucking car like belligerent fucking black dudes, but I understand that's where he was coming from.—Sandman

We went in to meet Tod Gordon, and we started talking. It was me who was chatting the whole time, not Mustafa. I was talking to him about what we could do, about why the Gangstas would work with his federation, and what we might just be able to expect from him. Namely, in the financial sense.

[New Jack] and I were laughing from the first time we met. He could crack me up like nobody else, and I think that went in reverse. There was cheap heat in SMW, and there wasn't going to be any of that up here. We just talked about what would happen in terms of our relationship. When I'd met him that afternoon, he was talking about his kids, his then-wife, a very soft, gentle New Jack, as opposed to the character he'd become later that day.—Tod Gordon

It didn't take long. We got things straight out fast and headed to our hotel. These guys looked like we might be able to take them at their word. We knew they could take us at ours.

Separated from the regular ECW crew and the fans, we took our first steps into character. This place was a new building, in front of new fans, but the work was the same. We'd been getting violent, doing street fights, going to the extreme for long enough now that we knew we could make this work. Just walk in there like we owned the place, and they might just give it to us.

We'd been in front of a bunch of white people screaming for our heads, too often because they didn't like the color of our skin. If nothing else, we could guess that this crowd would be a bit younger, a bit more diverse, a bit more open-minded about race. I wouldn't have to resort to cheap heat here, calling the fans names and cussing at them to get them to badmouth me. Now it was time to get over, hated or loved, by what we did between the ropes first and behind the microphone second.

We finally got to the arena. Now it was time to meet Paul Heyman, then known much, *much* better in wrestling as Paul E. Dangerously.

The interaction probably set a record for the shortest he'd ever been in.

"I'm glad you made it," he said. "I'm looking forward to working with you. This is what we're doing tonight...."

If we hadn't known how important he was, we probably would have forgotten the interaction about ten seconds after it ended. This guy would end up playing one of the most important roles in my career, but we couldn't have guessed that then.

Then again, we had many more important things to worry about over the coming hours.

12

ECW Debut

We didn't even know what ECW was. There wasn't social media back then, so you couldn't just call something up on the Internet and look at it. We're sitting in the parking lot, and I'm partying, celebrating our new home.—Mustafa Saed

We sat. We waited. We hoped. No talking right now, no interaction. I didn't even want to start thinking right then. This was not where you let the mind wander, afraid that it might go somewhere not in need of a visitor.

It was both a familiar place and a foreign land. The Gangstas would be doing the same stuff we always had in the ring, maybe with a few added notches of intensity, but we were in a new spot right now, in front of hundreds of people that *might* have known our names, but probably not much else.

We weren't sure, couldn't be. You never are, not that early in the game. We'd tried to have this session back in the hotel room, but this close to the action, little before the call of "Action," it can be a very different story. The fans might go nuts and cheer for us, they might boo us out of the building, or maybe give me a taste of my own medicine and not give a fuck about us, and that would be worst of all. But as fast as things can go wrong in wrestling, just like in anything else, we don't fix them until they break.

But even if the fans liked us, what about our new locker room crew? Newcomers aren't always made welcome in wrestling. Gordon and Heyman were about the only ECW folk we'd spent much time with by that point, and, sitting in a car outside the ECW Arena on that hot night in June 1995, waiting for our debut, we weren't going to make any great first impressions just yet.

As always, I didn't give a fuck. But this time, I had reasons not to even think about it. Inside the arena, Public Enemy was taking on Ian and Axl

54

Rotten. Moments after they'd win, their asses would belong to us. That was all I could afford to even think about.

Then thought turned to action. Enemy was celebrating their win, waving their title belts, waving their arms around. Fans were reacting a little bit. They'd been around for a while, but not everyone was into them. They weren't getting enough of a reaction, not like champs who are supposed to be over (having achieved a desired audience response).

Then two guys who looked like they'd be right at home in any ghetto in Philly—and there are quite a few—stormed in. They looked like maybe they had held up a 7–11 on the way over. One fellow had a bandana over his face. The other wielded a pipe, which was introduced to the back of Johnny Grunge's head.

That was me. While I gloated over Grunge's unconsciousness, Mustafa whomped hell out of Rocco Rock with some other weaponry. Pipe whacks, chair shots, and a ton of punches later, Mustafa slammed me onto Rock and right through a table. These guys were supposed to be the ECW champions, and we'd just made them our bitches for about five minutes. The crowd wasn't making too much noise, but no one was sitting; they couldn't believe that two guys could just saunter down the aisle and stomp the titlists into putty. A lack of vocal reaction isn't always a bad thing.

It was a dream come true. It felt like a time and place in history, and they couldn't take that from us.—Mustafa Saed

---

Finally, the cops showed up. For the first time in my life, I wasn't worried at all about them.

Paul had set it up so we'd actually be taken out and put in a police car. They took us around the corner and let us out. Fortunately, no one reported the cops for letting a couple of angry black men get away with crime.

We headed back to the hotel and started meeting the group. We had left one hell of a first impression on the fans, and now on the backstage boys. Everybody welcomed us pretty well. If our names, our looks, and our pasts hadn't showed the ECW crew that the Gangstas could get as extreme as anyone, they sure as shit knew now.

Then we flew back to Atlanta. But we were right back in town, and all the way into ECW, the very next weekend.

And a few days later, I found I'd made a different kind of "first" impression.

"One of my friends at church said they saw you getting arrested!" my mother blared at me into the phone. "I can't believe you're going up there and starting trouble already!"

"Fuck you!" I laughed.

But we were there now, at the place where we'd make a mark that no one would ever forget. ECW would be my home, my way of life, everything for New Jack for the next few years. All of ECW would know us very shortly; before long, the entire wrestling world would know my name as well, and they'd never forget it. ECW would push us as hard as any federation ever had or could, and I'd try as hard as I ever would. I was in a new world now, and I'd make it my own.

Like we saw so many other times over the ECW years—too often in hindsight—Paul E. did some stuff that was so far ahead of the times, things that other federations copied from him and then stole the credit for. One thing that helped us get over fast with the fans was blaring our theme, "Natural Born Killaz," not only before we came out of the dressing room, but during the match. It helped the fans get far into us. When fans heard Dr. Dre and Ice Cube's lyrics come roaring out ("Decapitating, I ain't hesitating, to put you in the funeral home!") in all their subtlety, they knew that the Gangstas were here, and that we'd mean some serious business.

The first time we came out, all the fans did was make every kind of noise. For our first match, I counted all of *two* signs. As we kept wrestling, I saw more and more signs all over the audience. People reacted to us, fast.

> *Their improvement was like leaps and bounds. I don't think anyone realized how good Jack could be on the mic. He just came off as being legit. It didn't seem like it was an angle. By being themselves, guys could extend themselves as the people they were in the ring. It was amazing to see all these little white kids in the audience give the X-signal for the Gangstas. We told them to keep wrestling like bad guys, but let [the fans] love you!—Tod Gordon*

And I found out pretty fast that these guys would have my back, and that made me want to have theirs when shit got real—and, as you'll see several times throughout this book, things got *very* real at times. As long as I was in ECW, I'd be part of a team, and you can't always find that in the business. I think if you ask around the crew in ECW, some of whom you'll meet in this piece, a lot of them will attest to the family nature of people who spent several evenings a week bashing each other's skulls in.

While I'd been in Smoky Mountain, I'd had a bit of an incident with a member of the Tennessee law enforcement community, a very frank discussion.

OK, I'd punched him. And then, by total coincidence, I'd forgotten to show up for court on the matter.

As I was getting ready to face some members of the Dudley family in a tag team match one night, a guy came to the front and told the ticket-sellers to let New Jack know that an old friend was there to visit him. Problem with that was that I didn't have any friends in that area. I knew something was up, and Paul did as well.

Yeah, the guy was a bail bondsman. He might have wanted my autograph, but it would be on a jail sign-in sheet.

Paul went to the guy, and, as few people could have, managed to convince him to let me finish my match before I turned myself in. This was going to be on TV, and no one wanted any legitimate legal action to get in front of the cameras. He assured the bondsman that he'd get his target for the night. As a former bounty hunter, I guess I should have felt some sympathy for the guy's plight. But I didn't.

As the match got going, of course things got extreme. The Dudleys and I went brawling down the aisle, then into the dressing room. As the bondsman waited for me to come back out, we battled towards the back door. We were away from the cameras now, but this show wasn't finished.

As we made it outside, a van just happened to be waiting there with its back door open. Far from anyone or anything inside, they conveniently decided to toss me into the van, and it sped right off. The law was going home empty-handed this night. I don't know if he got in trouble with his boss, or if Paul got in trouble with him, but my crew had helped me escape, without hardly knowing me at all. That's the kind of loyalty that kept me, and many guys like me, at ECW for a long time.

Still, I didn't get away, not all the way. On my own time, I went back to Tennessee, had my court date, paid my fine, put it behind me, and kept working.

As I'm sure you've read about all over the Internet, and will read about several more times throughout this book, sometimes things got out of hand in ECW, and I was involved more times than I wish.

Surrounded by a ton of screaming fans at a bar in Atlanta once, me and another wrestler were throwing down in the audience. Then he got an impromptu tag team partner: his wife. Mad at what I was doing to her man, she had the bright idea to jump in on predetermined action.

"Bitch, get out of the way," I muttered at her. Her poor, abused (by me!) hubby gave a start.

"That's my wife," he told me.

"I don't give a fuck if she's your mother," I shot back. "Tell her to get the fuck out of the way." He ran at me. I slammed him to the ground. Then I beat the stuffing out of him.

As the match got out of hand, wifey called the cops. I got the hell out of there. One of the owners, knowing who was the night's most valuable asset, assured me I'd be fine.

"We'll tell the cops that your name is New Jack," he said, "and that we don't know your real name." I got away, and never got in trouble for it.

For the next few years, I'd be smashing heads and other body parts with weapons that had never been used in any wrestling history, and I'd be feeling the same from others. Every week, I'd be jumping off balconies, crashing through tables, putting myself, and so many others, through punishment that would leave most people crippled, if they even had the strength to breathe.

As I'd find out, however, the ECW lifestyle could get even tougher *outside* the ring—in both the best and toughest ways of my career!

13

Ring Rats

The start of my ECW career ended up being the beginning of an end for me.

I'd gotten married about a year before, to a stripper I'd met at a strip club. This was my second go-round as a husband, and I thought it would work out. Maybe. I'm not really sure what was in my mind with that.

Anyway, she ended up hating wrestling. I wasn't going to quit. You can probably guess that this wasn't going to be an amicable separation.

We told each other to fuck off, and there I went. Straight to the Travel Lodge and eventually the Holiday Inn of Philadelphia, where the ECW crew would gather after a show.

And we weren't alone.

We'd go up and sit at the bar. Drink a little. Start bullshitting around. And then they'd come. The ring rats. The ECW groupies. The women.

The Friday night before the show, the women would arrive. Some lived there in Philly. Some slipped down from New Jersey. And others were from farther away. I saw a girl from Florida drive up to see ECW. By the time we'd get there, the place would be sold out. That's how many women would show up to, shall we say, help us heal up from our ring work.

It was always a big party. You'd go upstairs, you'd go to different rooms. We'd go from room to room, and sometimes we'd stay up all night. I'd go work out right after the party, and sometimes I was going four times a day.—Mustafa

It was like some kind of erotic college class. The ladies would show up on Friday night—sometimes they'd come to the show, sometimes they'd just wait there for us. Every show, you'd see some of the same women. Sometimes you'd see different ones.

They'd buy us cell phones, rent us cars, pay for our rooms, drive us around. They'd buy our drinks. Sometimes they'd buy or bring us drugs, although that didn't really start for me for a while into my ECW tenure.

If I showed up at the bar, there would be a line of them. I'd be sitting in the VIP section, and they'd pile up and come over to see me. Pretty soon, someone would come up to me and say, "New Jack, can I come to your room with you?" And usually I'd say yes.

So we'd start drinking, and then all the wrestlers would go up to the sixth floor, where we all stayed. The women would go from room to room, like sharks looking after food. Walking in circles, going all around, looking for wrestlers to pin down in bed.

I'd find one that I liked and give her the key to my room. She'd be there before me, and all bets went right out the door, along with her inhibitions. It was funny; these women went all around, looking for men, men that they'd always find sooner or later, but that's pretty much all they were there for. They didn't really talk to you that much. Sometimes they'd ask you about your family, ask you about the other wrestlers, but I was never one for that kind of conversation. I was pretty up front about it: "We're going to have sex, and then you're going to go to another room, and I'm going downstairs to get another woman." Sometimes that pissed the women off enough to leave right then and there, but usually it didn't. Usually they'd stay until it was through, and if they didn't, like I said, I'd just go and find someone else.

I'd average six a night. If you think I'm bragging, well, I might just be. To be fair, though, what guy wouldn't?

I'll never forget what it was like, standing there in my room, looking out the window as they left, back into boring character for the next few weeks. There would be a ton of them. Some walking home, some walking to their cars. It was like one of those movies about the apocalypse when a bunch of zombies join together to eat the people. Sometimes they would like to go to the next step with us, relationship-wise. Not too sure why I thought that a woman could sex her way into the heart of guys going around the block so many times.

"New Jack, I want to be your girl," one said once, all wistful and shit. Give me a fucking break. Did she think I'd take that as some huge declaration of one-night stand necessity?

"Bitch, the only reason you're here is because I'm on TV," I informed her, waking her ass up to reality. I didn't want to meet her family, all that crazy shit.

Well, maybe once in a while, you went a little farther. I know some guys did; some of them ended up married to a ring rat. I was living a few hours from Philadelphia once, and this girl named Carissa, who'd been with some of the other wrestlers, was staying with me. Well, a security guard friend and I went out to a bar and left her at my apartment.

We came back. And I couldn't believe it.

No, she didn't steal anything, didn't make a huge mess, none of that. She had taken some of that clay that you use to cover up cracks in the wall and gone all over my living room! The place looked like it had been polka dotted by a blindfolded guy with his hands tied behind his back.

"Bitch, what the fuck is wrong with you?" I demanded. I found out that she'd been snorting some coke that I had in my living room. I was almost relieved. Who the hell could get it into their head to do something like that in a regular state?

I got rid of her. D-Von Dudley was overly accommodating in taking her off my hands.

With the girls jumping around from room to room and bed to bed, we'd share stories, scouting reports on the gals, if you will. "She does *that*? Man, I want to get her next!"

Sometimes that worked. I was in my room one night, surrounded by a ton of people, all high and drinking, all kids of shit. As under the influence as everyone, including me, she turned to me.

"Can I go down on you?" she asked, sounding like an uncertain student asking a question in the middle of a class.

I let her do it. What, was I going to say no to that?

One girl used to collect used condoms. Don't ask me what she did with them. I didn't get with her, but she'd ask me for condoms that I and other guys had used. I always kept a box of condoms every time I went to the hotel, and it wouldn't take long before that box was slam-ass empty.

Look, I know that these women wanted New Jack, not Jerome. I was smart enough to realize that these women just wanted to jump a guy who was (sort of) famous, just so they could say to their friends that they'd slept with the guy on TV. Big deal. They offered, we (or at least I) accepted. ECW is the last place in the world to suddenly morph into a Puritan. I liked to have sex with a group of women, so I did. It didn't bother me. What would I care why they wanted to be with me? They did. End of the seduction spectrum.

Ironically enough, the toughest injury of my career—not necessarily the most painful, but sure as shit the most memorable—kept me from moving around with the women for a long time. I was working with Jack Victory one night, and he kicked me right in the manhood.

Wasn't the first or the thousandth time that had happened, but this one just kept hurting. I noticed some swelling—which, in all fairness, you normally wouldn't expect to be a problem!—with a huge knot on the side, and I went to the hospital. I'm betting this was one of the most memorable nights of that doctor's life.

He looked, he prodded, he even X-rayed. Then he gave me some sad, sad news, during which he could hardly brawl off a smile.

"Mr. Young," he said. "You have a fractured penis." Tough to imagine them making a cast for that kind of break!

It took some months to heal up, longer than some bones that have cracked. I couldn't have sex for a while.

Then it happened. I was shocked, but I probably shouldn't have been.

A woman I'd been with called me. "I think I'm pregnant," she said. What? Really? OK, this is tough. Our relationship had been almost entirely physical. I hardly knew this woman, and now we were going to have a kid.

Our daughter was born nine months later. But I'm not so sure she was the only one that came out of my ECW romps. I probably have a couple more kids out there that I don't know about. That's tough to handle sometimes, but there's not much I can do about it. What I am going to do, call up every woman I've ever been with and say, "How are you? By the way, have you had any kids that sort of resemble me over the past few decades?" I just don't worry about it.

14

New Jack's Kids

I've opened the door up about my kids, so we'll talk about them, but as much as I'll give you about everything else throughout this book, this is something I try to keep private, so we're going to keep it that way.

I became a father for the first time when I was living in Atlanta in the late '80s, when my old girlfriend had my daughter Brandy. Ashley is my daughter from the ring rat in ECW. Over the span of about two years, she, my son Kyle, and my daughter April came about. Well, after I left ECW, I had another son. Yes, I have kids with five different women, none of whom I was ever married to.

Being a father's been great for me. I've always managed, and I've always supported my kids, and I still do. How I did that, how I still do that, and how I always will do that is between me and them. My views on my ability as a parent are also between me and them.

Short chapter? You bet. Our business alone? Damn right. Now let's move on.

15

Using Drugs

If you're going to be a success in the drug dealing business, the first rule is simply to never get high on your own supply. You end up using all your own product, and the money that would have come with selling it. You make it easier for people to take advantage of you. You lose the rationale that any decent businessman has.

I'd always held tight to that mantra through my years of drug selling. Even when I was watching my wrestling colleagues use some of the worst—though sadly, most effective—forms of painkillers, I kept my nose clean in every sense of the word.

But I still liked my drink, always into the booze, and it's way too easy to switch from one substance use, if not abuse, to another. That, and, if you're as shitfaced as I was at the point I'm talking about, you're way too susceptible to suggestion anyway. One night, I went too far with the guzzling.

Crocked out of my fucking mind, I was leaning against a pole at the bar one night when one of the women from ECW strolled up to me.

"You all right, Jack?" she asked. I was about as far from all right as I'd been since I'd shown up in the company, and probably a long time before then.

"Sure," I slurred.

"You get high, right?" she continued. She might have been under something's influence herself, but I sure as shit wouldn't have known the first difference.

I honestly don't recall exactly how I responded, but it must have been something along the lines of, "Oh, hell yeah!" In any case, I ended up in a bathroom with Pitbull Number One.

He handed me a dollar bill with cocaine on it, and we laid a line out on the sink. Again, I was too drunk to really realize what I was doing. I don't believe I would have touched that stuff if I hadn't already been bombed out of my mind.

15. Using Drugs

It wasn't anything he did wrong, or that she'd done wrong. I don't think they saw New Jack as some vulnerable soul that they were trying to corrupt. Just doing something they thought was fun, and probably thought I'd like to join. I'd been asked to try it before, never pressured, and I'm pretty sure someone would have given me some if I'd just asked.

Strangely, my main memory of getting stoned for the first time is how much and how quickly it sobered me up. When you snort that shit up your nose, it goes straight to your brain, and you feel it almost before you finish exhaling. It gets you going. It makes your mind, your entire body, everything clear. You go into overdrive, and the feeling you get is enough to focus on everything around you—very, very easily. In a few seconds, my mind and body felt like I hadn't touched a drop of booze in forever.

So I went back to the bar and started all over. That much alcohol and drugs in my system at once, I could have overdosed at any point that night. I didn't think about it. Like I said, I couldn't think about hardly anything at all. Just how nice it was to get hammered twice in one night.

Before long, I started taking advantage of the new "medication." It brought me all kinds of excitement. It did for us all. It's something that you've never done before, and then you do it, and you know it's going to fuck you up, get you high, and make you ready to climb the walls.

And it made you get nuts during a match. Because you didn't feel shit. You got high as shit before a match, and you were ready to jump through the ceiling, or at least the fuck off of a balcony.

The matches would be intensified times ten. I'd do some shit, go out there snorted up, and I'd feel like fucking Superman. Sometimes Paul E. would run up to me as I was about to go out and wipe the coke off my nose.

It was an upper like crazy. You can wrestle for *hours* on it. You eventually crash, but you just go and do some more. You don't get tired, you just go. We'd fight in the audience, outside in the streets, behind the arena, in somebody's backyard. We'd be fighting near a street, and a car would drive by, and we'd throw each other into it. We did all kinds of weird-ass shit. When you're as fucked up as we were, you don't think, you don't feel. You just go and go and go and then you go some more.

One time, Jack was scheduled to do a five-minute interview, and on cocaine, he was on there for thirty-five minutes. It was one of the funniest things I'd ever seen!—Tod Gordon

---

I was doing it about every three weeks. I had a guy I knew in Philly, and he gave me everything I needed. It made me one popular mother-fucker in the dressing room. When I couldn't get the stuff, Paul E. would make sure I had what I needed.

Some guys took it a little too far. Once I walked into the dressing room at an event, and I saw three guys just sitting there. One of them drew a needle's worth of blood out of his arm, and the next one jammed it straight into his own. Then the other guy took some blood out of the second guy and injected himself with it.

I couldn't believe it.

"What the *fuck* is that about?" I could hardly keep from screaming at these assholes.

"Man, you need to try this!" One of them grinned at me, like he was offering a new dessert or something. "It gets you *so fucking high!*" I wanted to knock all of their heads together, or throw up from disgust right then and there. Sick fucks.

It got crazy enough that some of us started a poll in the locker room to see who'd OD next. I was on the list, and I would have put odds on my-self. Sadly, some of the other names on that list are gone now.

I'd even start to believe, even accept that I was probably going to die from drugs. I was going to take too much one night alone in my apart-ment, drop dead, and lie there for weeks before anyone happened by to find my body.

> *The drug scene was quite heavy, but when you're partying, rocking and rolling, you don't realize how much is going on until after the fact. There was a lot of that going on at ECW, having that mentality, that pressure to go, go, go, even if your body's hurt. You take a pain pill to get through the night, to get through the match, and the next thing you know, the two that you took before don't work, and now, three weeks later, you have to take four to take away the same pain you had that never got taken care of. Now you're taking something to go to sleep, and now you're in the cycle of getting addicted.—fellow ECW star 2 Cold Scorpio*

Sometimes, especially when we were away from the typical ECW grounds, we had to resort to some less conventional methods to grab up our cocaine. I was in New York once with some of my colleagues, and our stash had run empty. We hadn't had the goods for a while, and we were asking around. Desperate, we found some guys in front of a store in the middle of the hood. They told us about a reliable source right around the corner. They even described the guy to look for.

My pals waiting in the car, I went in the house, handed over a few hundred dollars, and came out with enough for us to make it through for a while.

Then I tasted it. It wasn't coke. Not even close. This guy was trying to fake out a group of guys who kicked each other's asses and ignored pain and suffering for a living.

Normally, you take that sort of thing as a write-off. Dealers don't exactly have an exchange policy, and you can't really call the cops and whine about someone selling you some fake cocaine. My friends wanted to take the safe way out and just drive away, maybe get lucky elsewhere, but I was too tired, too frustrated, too in need to wait.

I went back inside, and found my salesman in the hallway.

"Where's my money?" I inquired, getting more emotional by the moment.

"What do you mean?" he asked, either trying to play stupid or surprised someone would call him on his lack of ethics.

"You sold me this fake shit!" I informed him. Then I hit him in the head with the false product.

"No, partner, you...." he stammered.

"Partner, my ass!" I snarled. "Give me my fucking money!"

He sighed, and gave it back. I left. I don't recall where the drugs came from that night, but they arrived from somewhere. I was riding this train on a regular basis for years.

Once we were in Harlem, getting drugs in a high-rise. On the steps, there must have been thirty people in line. There was a door with a little slot. The slide would open up, and someone would ask, "What the fuck you want, white boy?" You slid in your money, and they gave you your product.—Sandman

---

Sometimes things got tough. Once I was getting dressed before a match, and stuck an eight-ball of coke in my pocket. I'm not sure if I meant to use it before the match or after, but either way, my stash was still there as I headed back to the dressing room. Then a guy came up to me with his young son.

"New Jack, my boy's your biggest fan," the father told me. "Can I buy your pants for him?"

I laughed, and told him not to worry about it. I went back, changed out of my fatigues, of which I really hadn't liked the color to begin with, and went back to hand them to the kid.

Back in the dressing room, I got ready to med myself off the pain.

Oh shit...

I jumped up like there was a rocket up my ass and hauled back to the crowd. This was one of the few times that I was fortunate to *not* be in the main event.

Fans saw me and crowded around, asking for autographs, photos, anything. I just prayed the kid was still there, and hadn't done any inspecting.

Trying to look nonchalant, I located the family, informed the kid that I'd left something a bit personal in the clothes, and asked to grab them back for a moment. The pants back in my hands, I turned away and reached inside. Then my hand closed on some lost treasure.

Feeling about fifty pounds lighter, I slipped my prize into my new pants, and grinned broadly as I handed the old pair back to the boy. It would be one of the finest eight-balls I'd ever snorted. The guys in the dressing room teased me about that one for years.

Other drug-based aspects, even in hindsight, weren't so humorous.

In the summer of 1997, I'd fronted some drugs to the Junkyard Dog. Even today, people still blame his drug issues for his not making it to the very top of the wrestling world.

Problem was, he'd never paid me for them. I guess he thought I was too stoned to remember, or that he'd get a free pass from me for being so well known in the business.

Yeah, no. When you owe me money, I'll remember you forever, and I don't give a shit if you've wrestled one match or one billion.

After he'd given me one excuse after another for about a year, I was at a cookout at Tommy Rich's house in Atlanta in early May 1998, getting ready for the *Wrestlepalooza* pay-per-view the next day. Then someone came to the backyard.

"Hey Tommy," the guy said. "JYD's on the phone." I was lucky enough to be standing there.

"Let me talk to him," I requested. I grabbed up the phone.

"Hey Dog," I said. "This is New Jack." I didn't hear anything for a few seconds.

"Put Tommy on the phone," Dog finally said.

"Did you get my money?"

"What money?" Oh yeah, now he was going to play dumb.

"Show up tomorrow at the pay-per-view and don't have my money," I said, "and you'll know what I'm talking about."

"Put Tommy on the phone, nigger!"

I informed Paul E. of my plans.

"How much does he owe you?" he asked sadly.

"No, you didn't *not* pay me back," I told him. "He did, so I'm getting it from him."

"Jack, I don't want you fighting Dog tomorrow." JYD wasn't even scheduled to have a match; he was going to show up and hope people remembered him for who he used to be.

"It's not going to be a fight," I assured him. "But I'm gonna get him."

The next day, I pulled up to the back of the Cobb County Civic Center. As I strolled in, Dog was standing there. I just looked at him.

"What?" he asked, trying to sound tough. "What?" I kept looking at him as I walked past to go put my bags down. Then I came back.

He was still looking at me when my pinkie ring smashed into his eye.

As he fell, I was already on him, punching the shit out of him. Fortunately for him, others were there to pull me off.

I hadn't lied to Paul E. There hadn't been a fight. A fight involves two people exchanging blows until one comes out ahead. Not this time.

"Goddammit, Jack!" Paul E. screamed in my face. "I was going to pay you!"

"I told you," I calmly explained. "You're not paying me."

When Dog came out for his appearance that night, some might not have noticed the bandage under his eye. That was from me. They also maybe missed that his shirt was too small. That's because the one he'd worn had gotten his blood all over it.

After the show, I was coming down from my own high. Dog came up to me.

"Jack, I'm trying to get a check cashed," he began.

"Motherfucker, it's almost midnight," I snorted. "How you going to get a check cashed? We're even. Just remember that I don't fuck with you no more." As it turned out, I didn't get a chance; a month later, he was killed in a car accident.

Like I just mentioned, I was zonked as hell that day myself. I clobbered Bam Bam Bigelow with a crutch, metal signs, a pan, even a Godzilla figure to the balls. Then he came back and rearranged my brains and vertebrae with chairs.

Bloody as hell but not feeling any of it, I led him up through the bleachers, then staggered up to a balcony, where I happened to find a guitar. Then I jumped off, and introduced the guitar to his cranium on the way down. Fans started giving the Gangstas' X-sign and chanting "ECW!"

A user himself, though not as hardcore as I was, he leaned over to me. "Jack, we're going home," he said weakly.

I started laughing hysterically. I felt like my heart was going to beat right out of my chest. Maybe I was going to have heart failure right there on the floor.

"I can't walk!" I snickered. "You have to carry me to the ring!"

"You motherfucker."

Throwing me over his shoulders, he hauled me up the aisle and between the ropes, smashed me with his finisher, and made for damn sure I didn't kick out. Then he hit me with a garbage can for good measure.

That was my normal life for about two years. It's funny in the saddest way; I did a shoot interview once talking about how, despite ECW getting blasted all the time for being so violent, so few of our wrestlers died compared to the WWE or WCW. My math may have been a little off then, but I sure as hell wish I could talk like that now. I can't, as Balls Mahoney, Axl Rotten, Chris Candido, both guys from Public Enemy, Bam Bam, and way too many others are gone now.

I'm sure that many people, including me, wouldn't have been shocked if New Jack had become a member of that sad fraternity, especially when I was at my highest. A few years later, I came as close as I could, but I'm still here to write this book.

16

Kayfabe

It sounds weird to say it, and looks strange here to write it, but the in-ring part of performing actually ended up being one of my easiest switches from Smoky Mountain to ECW. Getting slammed all over the ring, having my head smashed in by every foreign object you could think of, that was easy to carry over between federations.

Out of the ring was a whole separate story.

To a wrestling outsider, the word kayfabe might sound like a kid's toy or the latest makeup fad or something. To those who were in the business before me, it was an entire way of life.

In wrestling's olden days—as in, up through the early '90s, not *that* long ago!—everyone was supposed to believe that wrestling was as real as football, boxing, soccer, everything else. The fans needed to know that the grudges we took to the ring and the blows we threw there were full-blown real, and that the people we were in the ring were the same people we were outside.

Jim Cornette's the very epitome of a wrestling traditionalist. Kayfabe (or making things a "shoot," another name for maintaining wrestling's realistic mystique) has always been one of his trademarks in the wrestling business. Long before he gets to the arena, he's in character, whether he's a face or a heel, and he stays there until he's home. Like many from his day, and before his day, that's how he was as a character, and how he was as an owner.

When you worked for him, he made it clear he expected you to be as well. When fans showed up at Smoky Mountain, they were getting the type of show that had made wrestling such a worldwide phenomenon for decades.

Fans knew we were heels. They didn't talk to us. We stayed in character the whole time, and didn't get out until we were far from the arenas. You didn't shake hands with the fans, you didn't pose for pictures with fans, and you sure as hell didn't sign autographs or whatever else, if you

71

even came out of the dressing room at all. You were a heel in the ring, and you were just as big of one, though slightly less violently, outside of it.

If you're as bad as the Gangstas were, they weren't supposed to like you one way or the other, and you didn't try to change their minds. You want them to believe that they should act a certain way as well. If they're unlucky enough to see you outside of the ring, you make them want to get away and stay as far away as possible, or else they might end up getting what you just gave your opponent. They can get angry, get scared, whatever negative emotion you want them to feel, and keep it inside until the next show comes around, when they'll hopefully show up again to feel it again.

When we got over to ECW, though, it was everything but a different galaxy—except, of course, for the ring and mic work. A different federation with different co-workers, of course, but also in front of different crowds with different mindsets.

We'd do a show, then hit a hotel bar. And we couldn't believe it, but fans actually *came up and talked to us*! More amazingly, others who'd been in ECW before us were OK with this. Stunningly, Paul E. and Tod were fine with it as well! Was it actually acceptable to drop one's character in public?

Apparently so. Fans would walk up to us, shake our hands, tell us what they liked about the match and, crossing the line a bit, what they didn't. They'd say things like, "Damn, you did a great job pissing the crowd off tonight!"

It was totally foreign from Smoky Mountain. There, people cussed you out all the way into the parking lot, but they ran like hell as soon as you made eye contact. Forget about asking for autographs and photos; these people were too intimidated to venture within a stone's throw.

Here, the people that had just screamed for your head and cheered when you got creamed an hour before might be offering to buy you a beer.

I hadn't been in the business long enough to say which style I preferred—not yet. But I didn't take too long to adjust to the new place and its ways. It helped that New Jack's not all that different from Jerome, just kicked up a few notches.

It was strange, getting a taste of nostalgia so early on. People told me they'd been following me, and I'd only been in the business for a few years. I'd spent so little time around kayfabe that it ended up being pretty easy for me to leave it behind. I was fine knowing that the fans knew that there was a huge difference between the characters in the ring and the people outside.

16. Kayfabe

I wasn't experienced enough to realize it, but the business was changing, and we ended up having to change with it. Not saying I agree with this, but many from wrestling's past see the loss of kayfabe as the death of a loved one, the end of a golden era in the business. It's sad to see so many still feeling that way. I hope they're proud of how hard they worked to maintain wrestling's aura, and how successful they were for so long.

I, and most people my age and younger, just accepted kayfabe's death as inevitable. Especially when you're on the independent circuit, you can't be as heelish as you can in the ring. Now that fans have so much access to wrestlers, both all over the Internet and in-person when they can meet you at a show, you have to be nice, because you might be selling them something other than tickets. Today, wrestlers spend intermissions trying to get people to buy their pictures, figures, autographs, whatever else. We've got to be our own promoters, our own independent contractors. You can't blow people off anymore with your heelish persona, because they know better.

17

Taking Dives

The Gangstas had gotten off to a hell of a start in ECW, and we were rolling. Our opponents were on board, working hard to help us look good, along with the promoters, booking us higher and higher up the card. If we weren't going to be champions soon, we'd sure as hell be main-eventing, and that meant more money.

Then, for reasons that I don't even remember now, but that must have meant a hell of a lot back then, everything changed. Paul E. was upset with us about something, and I mean *pissed*. When Paul E. gets ticked off at you, he can carry a hell of a grudge. Night after night, show after show, we suddenly started getting our asses handed to us sideways and beaten down. For weeks, maybe even months, we hardly got a move in, forget about winning a match.

This shit went on and on, and suddenly all we could see was the bottom coming at us at high speed. We'd already burned a bridge at Smoky Mountain; if we got jobbed too far out here at ECW, we might not be able to rebound.

Looking at all the leverage that we didn't have, still being relative newbies and all, I sat Mustafa down for a conversation.

"I'm going to do something," I promised him, "that's going to make people not even remember who won the match."

"What?" he asked.

"Don't worry about it," I assured him. "Just trust me. Paul E.'s doing this shit, and I'm going to do something." I knew it would get over, and that the fans would be behind us 100 percent. Even a group of people who'd been exposed to the most extreme in the wrestling business (up to then) would go nuts for this one.

Next time we made it to the arena, we squared off with the Dudleys. While Mustafa and Bubba Ray went to war in and near the ring (the Dudleys have one of the largest, most diverse families in wrestling history), I battled D-Von through the crowds.

Soon, we made it to an area near the stands. I'm sure fans expected one of us to slam the other on concrete, bash our heads into a wall, something crazy.

But not this extreme. Nobody saw this shit coming.

I planted him on a table and strapped him down. Fans were confused here: What was I going to do? Tip him over? Carry him back to the ring?

Not even close. I started heading up a nearby staircase, up into the stands. Maybe I was chickening out and running away, tying him up to get a head start.

I strolled up an aisle in front of the crowd, soon reaching a balcony in the middle. They probably thought I was going to wave goodbye and run like hell.

Then they realized that I was right above him. But I was about two stories up; what the hell could I do? Throw something at him?

I climbed on top of the balcony. I raised my arms. That's when they finally started to realize what was going on. Many of them probably figured New Jack was a bit off, but none thought I was this far gone. I was proving everyone wrong. I couldn't hesitate. I couldn't take any time to consider anything. I was going to do this shit.

I leapt off, crashed down on D-Von and the table, and sent the crowd up like a living wildfire. People absolutely lost their shit, screaming, yelling, jumping on each other. Lying there, I knew I'd done something brutally unforgettable.

I was right. The Dudleys won the match, but the whole rest of the match, people never stopped chanting, "New Jack! New Jack!"

People might have thought I was working on a dare, or maybe just exercising some kind of sadistic pleasure, getting something out of my system, a one-time thing that I'd never be nuts enough to do again.

I did it again. Show after show, I was taking one dive after another, dropping dozens of feet in the air and landing on my opponent, or a bare floor if he moved. What can I say? I just liked doing it. Not to say that's the most rational interest, but I enjoyed flying through the air, even if every landing was a crash.

The important thing was, the chants kept growing. More and more people, who might have moved away when we started losing, were behind us. One night in the dressing room, Paul E. took a humble stroll up to us.

"I give up," he admitted. "You're out there doing that diving shit so much, they don't even remember the finish." The grin on my face was nowhere near the one I felt on the inside. I'd gotten us back over, and now we were moving up again.

But all that ended up turning me into a role model of a different kind, one I never attempted or wanted to be. Right around that time, this garbage called backyard wrestling was starting to take off. You started seeing videos of guys with more dreams than brains jumping off roofs, building their own rings, setting each other on fire, smashing one another with huge pieces of glass, and whatever else, all over the place.

I thought it was ridiculous to see that, sickening to see people doing that shit to themselves. But it became sadly clear that people like me had accidentally set an example. ECW's action was starting to get imitated, and with obscenely high jumps becoming a part of backyard wars, it was a safe bet that too many people were trying to emulate the spirit of New Jack.

Then I found out how right I was. People started coming up to me with videotapes, saying, "Hey, can you watch this video of me jumping off a roof?" It was like they wanted my approval.

I was always like, "Sure!" I'd watch it, laugh at them, and then find them and tell them to have fun, but try not to get hurt. At least, not hurt any worse than they already had.

I can think of some things I'd rather be known and remembered for, but it looks like my balcony dives will always be part of the New Jack legacy. But that's not how I started off—if I had, I wouldn't have gone anywhere in the business. I learned to wrestle from Ray Candy and others, and I focused on it for my first few years in the business, in Georgia, in the USWA, and even for most of my run with Jim Cornette. It wasn't until I was almost at the end of my Smoky Mountain run that I even touched on the extremism that would become New Jack's persona.

I'll never forget one night in ECW, when I was scheduled to go one-on-one with Tommy Dreamer. We had a brief discussion in the dressing room, and I strolled out to the ring, my garbage can in hand. Then Dreamer got the mic.

"Hold up, New Jack," he told me. "You've been coming out here with that garbage can, beating people with shit for years. Tonight, we're going to show these people something different. Tonight, we're going to *wrestle*."

I did a triple-take, a shocked look on my face. The fans couldn't believe it either. New Jack without the E in ECW? Crazy!

Then we locked up. I snatched Dreamer in a headlock. Then he ran off the ropes, and I hit him with a shoulder tackle, armdrag, hiptoss.

And the crowd went nuts. They couldn't believe it. What had I been hiding from them for years? Had someone invented a cloning machine and made a newer, cleaner New Jack?

No, just something I didn't get to show very often. And sadly, I wouldn't get to show it too often for the rest of my career—very little in ECW, sometimes later in NWA Wildside, maybe a bit in TNA.

When I still see that backyard bullshit, I think it's funny, though not always ha-ha funny. Yeah, it's darkly humorous to see someone jumping off a roof and crashing through two tables and a plate-glass window while his buddies record it, thinking he's going to get anywhere in the business because of that stupid-ass shit. You just can't help but laugh at people like that, because people like that are down on their knees begging to be mocked. I still laugh at that garbage, especially if I'm already in a good mood.

But sometimes it makes you feel funny like the way your stomach feels funny when it's about to toss something back out the north exit. You feel sick. You feel sad. Seeing that, you just get depressed that, yes, there are people, too many people (one would be too many), that believe this. People whose viewpoint is so screwed that they do this because they want to get into wrestling, or because they might actually think it's fun. You'd think that by now, usually at or near adulthood, they'd have figured out that human invincibility doesn't exist, but too many of them keep feeling like they need to try it out.

I'd never tell anyone not to try to get into wrestling; there's millions of reasons not to, but it's not up to me to tell someone they can't make it. But if they want to, backyard stuff is the last way to do it. People can do that stuff and show it to a promoter, and nine times out of ten, the promoter's not going to give it a second look or thought. And the one who will might pay you $20 to do something nuts in front of about ten people and then put it on the web for his own personal gain.

It takes work. It takes time. It takes training. The up-and-comers need to wrestle first, and then try to get extreme. Go to a good trainer (honesty's not always easy to find in wrestling!), spend time getting the basics, learn some more about what to do between the ropes. Everyone who's ever made it in the business, even those who ended up being known for being extreme, started off the same way. It's the same process as moving up through any other organization, and no one picks it up right away. You just keep working, keep trying, keep learning, one move, one bump, one match at a time.

And the rewards come from everywhere, I'll tell you. For a guy who preaches about not worrying about titles, something else, something you might be surprised by, meant a *hell* of a lot to New Jack.

About a year into my tenure at ECW, some guys came by and had us pose for a ton of pictures. They took close-up headshots, pictures of us posing and looking scary, everything. Not long after that, I strolled into a local toy store.

Walking down one of the aisles, I was glancing around everywhere. Then I saw it. Actually, I saw me. I was an action figure. There I was, hanging on the wall, joining the ranks of G.I. Joe, He-Man, and the Transformers!

I grabbed one. Not good enough. I snapped up every single one I could see. I must have had about twenty of them in my hands.

At the register, the cashier, not surprisingly, looked a bit uncertain.

"Why did you buy all the same figures?" she couldn't help but ask.

"This is me!" I excitedly spouted. Now her face changed to sarcastic suspicion. A human form was standing there, holding his own toy creation.

"Look at it!" I told her. Then a manager came forward, and he looked about as shocked as I had been, in a similar way.

"Are you New Jack?" he asked. Luckily, I'd run into a fan. The cashier looked at me again.

"Shit!" she exclaimed. "This *is* you!" Now I got a bit of preferential treatment.

"We're going to give you a discount," the manager said, maybe to score points with a celebrity or apologize for his employee's attitude.

I took them home and hung them up all over my house. Over the years, about every time someone new came to visit, my collection would mysteriously shrink. I think I have about three left.

It was hilarious. We'd be at a show, and the fans would be sitting in the stands, ready for us to come out and draw gallons of blood. Backstage, you had a bunch of grown men arguing over whose action figure was the most realistic.

Over the years, I've become a few more figures. It's one of the greatest things, to see yourself hanging from the shelves of a toy store. It gives you the strangest sense of accomplishment.

18

New Weaponry

The drugs, the women, the parties, everything had finally gotten perfect for us in ECW. We were getting along great with everybody (almost, as you'll see soon) behind the scenes, Paul and Tod seemed to be impressed with our work ethic (took them long enough!) and, most importantly, the fans kept coming to see us and cheer us, whether we hoped they would or not.

In wrestling, any good promoter listens to the fans before anything else, or the guys who might be over stop trying and probably find somewhere else to go. Believe this—if a rival promoter has the first bit of sense and foresight, he'll be able to see that if one of your guys or gals is over, and you're not pushing him or her right, he'll snap your performer up, because the majority of his work is already done; the wrestler's already in great with the fans, so all the promoter has to do is put him in the same form and let him win a few matches. All the people that wanted to cheer your guy all the way to the top are now cheering for him in another spot, and someone else is benefitting!

Remember when everyone called WCW pure genius for putting together that NWO squad and letting them run roughshod over the federation for (in hindsight) a much longer time than they should have, and it ended up being one of the things that killed off one of the oldest promotions in history? Garbage! WCW didn't do anything smart with that—they just took a bunch of guys that the WWF had already made famous, put them all on the same team, and let them win more than they should have. It didn't take any skill to just repackage a bunch of guys the fans already knew.

What takes talent is the ability to make new stars. Whether it's taking a guy that the fans already know and putting him in a new package that makes them say, "Damn, we never realized how great this guy could be!" (like the WWE did with Stone Cold Steve Austin, in wrestling for years before he exploded), or taking someone the fans have never seen before and making them stand up and say, "Wow!"

That's the position that ECW was in for so long. Its fans might have heard our names once in a while (not just the Gangstas, but most of ECW), maybe saw us before sunrise on a UHF-channel show or something, but chances are they didn't really *know* who the hell we were. That's why, when the Gangstas first came out of the audience that night, no one chanted our names or even responded much at all at first. We were strangers in a new land. It would be up to the wrestlers and the people that made them behind the scenes to make the fans want to keep watching.

One way to do that was to let the fans get closer to the action than any other federation would have had the balls to try. Wrestlers fighting in the audience would become pretty common in the larger federations over the next few years, but it started with us. In other federations, fans that reached over the guardrail to get involved would probably get ejected immediately, even arrested; in ECW, it was normal.

If I'd gotten to ECW a few months earlier, I'd have been there for that legendary incident at *Hardcore Heaven* the August before, when Terry Funk, on a whim, asked the audience to throw him a chair during a brawl with the Public Enemy. About ten seconds later, the ring was covered in a pile of chairs with the Enemy buried underneath. I love watching that clip on the Internet.

My promos, so I've been told, have always done a pretty good job bringing the fans into the match. The fans themselves gave me an extra chance to get them involved.

An effect that had been rising ever since ECW began, you'd see people standing in line outside to get in holding all sorts of weapons. They'd have crutches, keyboards, computers, frying pans, monitors, guitars, bats, all kinds of shit. It was like they'd been thinking about having a garage sale or taking a few bucks out of a pawn shop, but they'd just decided to see if these objects could be used to concuss someone instead!

Even security would be smart enough not to let the fans actually carry the "weaponry" into the building; they'd put it in a garbage can. But not for the dumpster out back; when that thing got full, they'd bring it to New Jack!

I'd ditch the shit that I didn't want, but when that match started, the leftovers were going to the ring with me. Nothing made the fans' night like seeing me take something they'd brought and put it through someone's cranium. That was something they'd remember. Something they'd go home and talk about, maybe to their fellow wrestling fan friends who'd want to bring something themselves at the next show.

18. New Weaponry

When other federations did a "hardcore" match, it was a special event. The WWE even had to single out a "hardcore" champion to let people know that, at least for the next match, the shit was gonna hit the fan. In ECW, shit hit the fan when the very first bell rang, and didn't stop until the main event ended!

One of the funniest things I ever saw with this was right around Thanksgiving one year. I was digging through the can of offerings before the match when my hand suddenly hit something ice cold. I reached down and pulled out the item.

It was a frozen turkey. I actually had to put it down from laughing so hard. Of course, I took it to the ring that night, and made for damn sure to show it off before I hammered someone with it. The fans got as big a kick out of it as I did, and I could see the referee, ring announcer, and even the other wrestlers hiding their faces to keep from breaking character too. I just couldn't help but think that there was a family sitting at home for Thanksgiving dinner, pissed off because their kid had brought it to me! Can you imagine if that kid was sitting in the crowd with his parents, who had just found out the hard way that I was waving their stolen poultry?

If you've ever looked into the name of New Jack in any detail, you've probably run across quite a few of the individual, *cough, cough,* incidents that I've gotten into. Some of them happened in the ring, some of them backstage. Some were predetermined that didn't go as planned.

I typically get made out to be the bad guy in these matters, usually because there have been so many of them. People wonder that if one guy can get into so many donnybrooks with so many different people, there must be something wrong with him.

It's just not like that. Throughout this book, I'll be telling the side of those stories you haven't heard, not all the way. I'm no choirboy, never have been, but I've been caught in the wrong place in the wrong time as much as anyone. It's just that most people can get into situations like that without having them thrown in front of anyone with a keyboard.

As much as you think you know about New Jack, you haven't heard the whole tale about any of these incidents, these situations that people want to make a part of my infamy. When New Jack has been accused of crossing the line between reality and sports entertainment, there are parts of every single incident that finish making up the whole truth.

Like the one we'll discuss now.

19

Oct. 6, 1995—
A Dance with Dudley

I knew my face was about to get bashed in, but I was OK with that for now. It's just a part of the business. You hurt someone, they're going to hurt you, even if it was their fault they got hurt. It's wrestling's version of an eye for an eye, except that both of them end up blackened.

I'd called the spot well ahead of time, telling Dances with Dudley to duck my clothesline and keep moving. But when I shot him off the ropes, he only put his head down a little bit, and I'd smashed him in the bridge of the nose.

"Jack," he moaned, "I think you broke my nose." The blood gushing from it gave his theory some credibility.

"I'm sorry, dude," I told him, hiding my speech from the fans like wrestlers have to learn early on, "but I told you to duck."

Fine, fine, so he'd get me back. Nothing new. Getting hit never bothered me, as long as it was within the match confines. Once, Sandman and I had gotten into it in the ring. He'd smashed me in the head with his Singapore cane, and I mean *hard*. Then I got him back, blasting him with a chair so hard that the chair almost folded.

"Jack, what the fuck?" he grunted as we rolled around the ring, holding our heads.

"We're even, you fuck!" I mumbled back. "Fuck you, my head hurts!"

"Sorry, man," he stammered. We finished the match and drank and drugged afterward.

With Dudley, things wouldn't have such a happy ending. He started punching me, and the match slowed down. Much more of this would give our personal issue away to the crowd.

"OK, we're even," I told him between slugs.

"No," he asserted. "This shit ain't over with!" I guess he thought I was going to let him knock the hell out of me until he was satisfied, but that's not how it worked.

"Don't forget who's going over!" I snarled. I cut off his attack, then took him out (work-wise) for the pin.

I hadn't worked with this guy too many times, but we hadn't had any problems, so I thought this night in the tiny Pennsylvania town of Jim Thorpe wouldn't cause any trouble. People who get personal in the ring bring some trouble on themselves. Dances, one of the several Dudleys sprinkled all over wrestling, was about to make a universal mistake in the business.

I rolled out of the ring, but he wasn't finished.

"It ain't over!" he yelled at me. "Not over, fucker!"

I don't allow that from anyone, especially a guy who's going to throw a fit with me over one missed blow in wrestling. You threaten me, you better be ready to follow up—I will be.

I made it back to the dressing room at a slightly faster rate of speed than was necessary. I stepped into the small, dark room, stepped behind the door, and pulled out a nightstick I carried. This wasn't a gimmicked weapon or a worked match; there would be no referee or security guys to jump in and break us up. Some people might say I was overreacting, taking things too seriously, but I don't give a fuck. Nobody's going to threaten me and walk away, especially not in front of people that might try to get over on me the next time we're in the ring.

I was through the locker room door first, and I looked to my left, and New Jack was right there. *He blew right past me and into Dances.—Lou "Sign Guy Dudley" D'Angeli*

He stepped through the door. As soon as he was all the way in, I tried out my new finisher—my nightstick to his brainstem. I smashed him with it, then beat the shit out of him any way that I could. If others hadn't run in and broken it up, I don't know how things would have ended.

There were a million guys trying to pull them apart, which almost started a million other fights. I got pushed right out of the way by people much bigger than me. We saw these guys killing each other in a very small space. It was thirty-five guys back there, and all kinds of shit happening.—Lou D'Angeli

---

Pretty soon, everybody in the room was trying to get between us, and I was hitting anything that touched me. Mikey Whipwreck was there, of course Mustafa was, along with anyone but the people in the ring.

Then Taz, who always tried to pass himself off as a locker room big guy, decided to get in my face, like he had any room to say a word.

"New Jack," he said, like some sort of pint-sized mediator, "you know you were wrong for that." Right or wrong, he didn't have any business talking that kind of shit to me. Like everyone else, I always ignored that short piece of shit, but that was about to change.

"You want a piece of me?" I blasted. Then I roared at him, and someone grabbed me. As I was escorted out, I saw Dudley laid up in the corner, his head bleeding more than his nose had just a few minutes earlier.

All hell broke loose in that dressing room. I was off to the side, talking to somebody else, and then suddenly Jack was fighting with this guy. At first, no one knew what to do, because they'd never had that happen there before. Most of the time, they'd just talk about each other. They'd get on TV and say stuff about each other, but we didn't really see anybody fight. I thought that Jack was going to get him the next time we got in the ring, but Jack didn't wait that long.—Mustafa Saed

---

Back at the ECW Arena the next night, Mustafa and I squared off with the Eliminators. Then Paul E. came up to me.

"Jack, we're going to have to send you home for a few weeks," he said.

I didn't care. If I had to go home, I had to go home. It kind of pissed me off that Dances never got any punishment.

The whole locker room wanted to kill Jack, because none of our workers ever did anything like that. I think that if they saw he was cool with me, they'd be cool with him. I went to a diner across the street, and there were a couple of other guys there that wanted to kill him. He came over to my table, and said, "Can I sit with you?" We ate together, and people let up on him. If I was cool with him, they'd be cool with him.—Tod Gordon

---

I was home for a month, and guess what I was doing? I was back hunting down some bounties. Never caught or hurt anyone else, but that was a fallback for me in case money got tight. I didn't really stay in touch with my ECW friends, but one day, my pal Scorpio pulled up to my place in a van.

"Still suspended?" he asked.

"Yeah."

"Would you babysit my kids?" he asked hopefully. I looked in the back of his van. Five small pairs of eyes stared back at me.

Me, looking after a group of kids? Damn, was every other person on the planet busy? I'd just beaten the hell out of a grown man for getting in my face; can you imagine what I'd do to some little brat?

"Fuck no!" I laughed. In any case, I was back with Mustafa soon after, and everyone moved forward.

When that bell rings, your friendship goes out the window. When we wrestled, it was a hard-hitting brawl. Once, he stabbed me in the nose with a fork, and I had to get five or six stitches after the match was over.—Scorpio

---

I'm sure Dances is still pissed at me (I would be if he'd done that to me), but he was gone a few months later. Ironically, him getting hurt the next year—from a leg injury, not by me—opened the door for D-Von Dudley to show up in ECW. He and Bubba Ray would form one of wrestling's top tag teams of the past few decades, racking up the titles in ECW, WWE, Japan, everywhere.

While we're talking about the Dudleys, I want to address something else that's always all over the Internet, with people writing all kinds of garbage and stuff that's miles from the truth. There's always been this huge rumor that I have this issue with Bubba Ray and D-Von. But, per usual when outsiders get involved, it's all been blown out of proportion, and it's been over for a long time.

First off, I admit that I never thought much of Bubba Ray, before or after this incident. He and I just were two people that were far apart. Just rubbed each other wrong. But D-Von and I were tight. We hung out all the time and I even laid down in the ring for him a couple of times. When the Dudleys headed off to the WWE in 1999, I was rooting for them, or at least for D-Von.

But that's where the problems started. First off, they started coming to the ring dressed like me, which pissed me off; these guys had been over like crazy for years in ECW, and they didn't need to steal my image to keep going.

But then they went further—too much further. When ECW fans heard a whistle, turning into the sound of a missile dropping, they knew New Jack was going to appear. From the dressing room, through the audience, out from under the ring—I was coming.

Then the Dudleys took that as well. They stole my opener and put it on their WWE entrance music. Music that had helped make my career was now getting someone else over, in front of a much larger audience.

We had some heat over that, and for a long time. But I might have been over-blaming here; newcomers to the WWE, the Dudleys weren't able to say no to anyone. It may have been someone else's idea, which became more than an idea, for them to use my gimmicks.

Over the past few years, it's gotten better, but probably too slowly to be considered significant progress. I see them sometimes and we speak, but it's never gotten anywhere near what it once was. That used to bother me, but I don't worry too much about it anymore. I just keep going forward. Some have been there with me, and others haven't. It's how any business works.

Our first months in ECW had zipped by, although we were hitting the drugs, bars, and ladies as much as the bumps that we didn't have too much time to consider it. Everywhere we went in ECW, we were hated. People got over just from fighting us; our opponents didn't have to do anything other than yell, "We're kicking the Gangstas' ass tonight!" and the crowd would go berserk. We were cool with Public Enemy as people, but they only looked good in the ring because Paul E. was so talented at hiding people's weaknesses—and, yes, he did that with us.

But the fans had a surprise for us. Our fanfare was about to take a 180—not as strong as a 187, but it made one hell of a difference. It was nothing we did, nothing we said, no one we beat.

Just six months after being booed, jeered, and cussed out like crazy in our ECW debut, the Gangstas were about to grudgingly go good, and it would be the easiest thing we'd do since we'd arrived.

I honestly don't remember what ECW's original plan was for the Gangstas when we arrived—whether they hoped we'd be the company's top heels and be booed like crazy, with fans paying to hope we'd get lynched (like in Smoky Mountain), or the badass heels that people couldn't help but cheer for. Or anything else. But, as it would do far too many times during my career, Jerome's legal issues would interfere with New Jack's push.

And, per usual, I'd find a way to turn those negatives into positives.

20

New Jack Goes Good

Public Enemy was heading off to World Championship Wrestling, and we had to lie down for them in the main event of the *House Party* pay-per-view a few days into 1996. Doing that at all, let alone in the event payoff, probably made WCW look stronger than us, but I didn't give a fuck at the time.

Then my past came up again and yanked me right back down. I guess I'd gotten so caught up in the ECW fanfare and parties that I thought I could finish running away from this, but I was wrong. The law never leaves you behind—the will get you to make even, with interest.

Sleeping off another wild night, I got a sick wakeup call in every sense from my attorney. There was a warrant for my arrest for selling some drugs when I'd been down in Smoky Mountain, and now I was going to pay up.

I wasn't worried. First off, I'd be in county jail, which would be the Taj Mahal next to where I'd done time way back when. Second, Paul E. assured me I'd be back in less than a week. I'd go down to Atlanta, turn myself in, then he'd get me out, and I might miss a show.

That second part? Didn't happen. He didn't show. Instead of a few days, I was stuck down in the Clayton County Jail, right down the road from Atlanta, for *nine weeks*. OK, so it wasn't another year, and, no, it wasn't as hard as doing hard time over a decade before, but jail's jail. My friends, even my enemies, in ECW, were up north partying and wrestling, and here I was, staring out from behind the bars, thinking about how many ways I could make Paul E. painfully scream in payment.

But when I was there, something very weird was happening. Neither me nor Mustafa nor even Paul E. realized or could have predicted it, but the fans sure as hell did. Mustafa didn't work well without me. He wasn't over as a singles wrestler, and never had been—unless he was working *against* me, which didn't happen for a while.

To be fair, I had to think long and hard about whether I wanted to come back and work for Paul E. Did I really want to work for someone like that? Sure, I was still going to get paid, more than anyone else would give me right then; a guy with a record like this would have a tough time breaking in at a new arena. That, and I could redirect all the frustration I had with him, and take it out on my opponents. I didn't waste time with that.

Paul E. had temporarily brought in a few guys called the Headhunters to make the ECW guys look good, then leave. They didn't beat anybody while they were around, and weren't in the company for three weeks. But at a TV taping in early March in Queens, they jumped Mustafa and were stomping him into asphalt.

Then "Natural Born Killaz" hit, and the crowd went absolutely fucking crazy. I came roaring through the crowd, heavily armed, of course, and wrecked shit all up. Mustafa joined in, and the fans yelled as loud for us as they ever had for the faces.

I tried to hold down the fort until Jack got back. I had been wrestling singles for a long time when I first started. You have to keep your mind straight in this business; I was going to keep the angle going until he got back, and then we'd have some fun! We knew we'd have no problem getting the crowd back when he returned.—Mustafa Saed

---

Then I got a mic to cut a promo that finished changing our direction.

"I've been gone for a couple of months," I reminded the crowd, "and I actually missed you motherfuckers!" Only in a place like ECW could that be a declaration of the heart.

But it's actually funny; for one of the first times in my ECW career—hell, most of my wrestling career—I was serious. I *had* missed the fans, though not really because I liked them, or they me. I had missed them because being away meant I wasn't getting paid. I had missed getting wild in front of them, hearing them scream about what a scumbag I was, but the check was the main object.

They didn't care. Chants of "New Jack, New Jack" started blaring around the arena, louder than my entrance music had been. I'm really not sure what I was feeling at this point. I don't think I was especially happy or sad about what was going on, but more just excited about being part of something big, and being the reason it had happened.

We went backstage. Paul E. was in my face in about five seconds. It really didn't bother me to see him pissed right then and there.

"You realize what you just did?" he demanded. "You turned yourself into a face. You were the biggest heel I had in the locker room, and now you turned yourself into a face!" Yeah, he'd been building us to beat up his faces for nine months, and I'd flipped us around in a few shouted sentences!

Like I said, I was OK with Paul E. being mad, at least at first. But back in the familiar world of women and booze a short while later, I was a little worried. How could I get the fans to cheer me some more, not only after pissing them off here, but in Smoky Mountain, which I'm sure many of them remembered? If I couldn't, and they stopped cheering, would they take me seriously as a heel again?

Either way, could I get enough of them to come pay to watch me?

21

Jack vs. Austin and Pillman

I'm sure there are a few here and there that would disagree from over the years, but I think I'm a pretty easy guy to work with. I've never held back anyone, not on purpose, or kept anyone from getting anything they didn't deserve. I've never had a problem putting anyone else over, again, if they'd earned it.

Having said that, I don't claim to be the poster child for popularity either. You'll hear all kinds of stories about how I keep to myself in the locker rooms, only sharing my social life or my personal life with people who stuck around long enough for me to let them in. That's not to say that this is normal or good for everyone, or for most people. It's just the way I've always been, and I think I've discussed enough from my past to justify that kind of attitude in this book.

Authority isn't something I'm too high on either. Taking orders, being a "Yes man," being a follower, has never been for me. I'm not a guy that you can really approach and say, "OK, here's what we're going to do, and you just follow me and we'll be OK!" Throughout this book, you'll hear stories of people that tried that tactic and ended up paying dearly. Very dearly, and very, very painfully. I wrote the first chapter of that aspect of my career—which now becomes the next chapter of my autobiography.

Back in Smoky Mountain, some guy had started milling in with the wrestlers, telling us all some story about how he was an agent for ECW, looking for talent. Follow him, and we'd be the brightest new stars of a company that was going to make WCW and the WWF (now WWE) look like cavemen and has-beens!

I'm not really sure who he thought he was fooling. I knew, and everyone else knew, that this guy was full of bullshit up to his forehead. We were pissed at him, but we didn't worry much; he wasn't worth that kind of trouble.

21. Jack vs. Austin and Pillman

Most of us figured we'd never see him again, that he'd piss someone off somewhere and either get his ass kicked badly enough to never show it again, or lie to the wrong people and get blackballed from every arena, armory, bingo hall, hotel, bar, and anywhere else that hosts a show. So we all got a little surprised that night in late March 1996 at the ECW Arena.

The night before, at a show in Reading, Stevie Richards was wrestling Rob Van Dam, and RVD accidentally kicked Stevie in the face and broke his orbital bone. The next night, me and Stevie were supposed to wrestle the Gangstas, and Chad Austin came in to substitute. Stone Cold Steve Austin was the hottest thing in wrestling at that time, so we called him "Lukewarm" Chad Austin.—The Blue Meanie

Meanie was even newer to ECW than I was, and Mustafa and I liked him a lot. He was working hard, trying to make something happen for himself, a friendlier fellow you won't meet. He and I knew that we could trust each other in a great match and then drink at the bar afterward. This Austin guy, though, he'd be a very different story.

Like what would happen in the infamously legendary Mass Transit incident later that year—yes, you'll get the full story to that relatively soon—Austin came to me and said he wanted to do this, to do that, to get color, fight into the audience, all sorts of crazy shit. I knew his name, but I wasn't sure he knew exactly who the fuck he was, or who he was speaking with. I went to see Meanie for a quick chat. Then I sat down with Mustafa.

Before the match, New Jack came up to me and said, "Meanie, me and Mustafa are working with you and this guy Austin. I don't want to hurt you, so stay with Mustafa." They didn't have to tell me twice.—The Blue Meanie

The Gangstas' finish started off as me climbing to the top rope, then Mustafa throwing me off and me headbutting the guy. But Austin had pissed me off so bad that we needed to do something else. Something convincing. Mustafa asked me what I had in mind, and I didn't know just yet.

Then it hit me. Just not nearly as hard as it would hit Austin—and, as it would turn out, so many more later on.

Austin got his wish, but not in the way he wanted. While Mustafa and Meanie had a by-the-numbers brawl in the ring to keep the crowd focused on the real event, I was beating the hell out of Austin all around the ring and into the audience, smashing him with chairs, crutches, everything. This wasn't quite what he'd had in mind.

Mustafa slammed Austin to the ground, and I headed up. But I wasn't leading with my skull this time. I had a chair in my arms, and I tried to smash Austin's head right through the mat. No one knew that the exact move would become my finisher, or that it would soon be known as the 187.

If you watch that match, it's like two separate matches going on at the same time. It's like we're in a castle with a moat around us, New Jack destroying Austin like he was a shark. That was a very surreal moment, a welcome-to-ECW moment.—The Blue Meanie

---

I pinned him. Then I picked up the chair and started smashing the hell out of him some more. He started trying to wave me away, but that wasn't going to work. I whacked him as many times as I goddamn well wanted.

Time to tell the crowd just what the fuck was going on here. My promos, which I never rehearsed, always had a strong sense of realism to them. People like to accuse wrestling of dancing all over the line between sports and entertainment, but I was going to set those people straight.

"This ain't entertainment," I pontificated. "If any of you motherfuckers think that that little punk bitch [Austin] just got entertained, you go talk to him." It turned out that Austin's leg ended up snapped. Big deal. What was he going to do, come and kick my ass? Sure.

With that much offense, that much aggression, and that kind of mic time, everyone had to know that the Gangstas had impressed certain people enough to move to the next level in ECW—like, say, a title shot!

Yeah, I still didn't give a fuck. But it wouldn't be long before things got out of control again, and this time the fans wouldn't see it.

Don't ask me what was going through this fool's mind the next June. I wasn't doing an angle with Brian Pillman, didn't hardly know the guy. So the next June, he came miles out of left field when he grabbed a microphone in front of the ECW Arena crowd and uttered the un-magic words "Niggas with Attitude!" about the Gangstas.

People tried to excuse it, saying he was zonked on painkillers from his recent car crash, or that he was referring to the rap group N.W.A, or that he was just trying to be one of the guys. I didn't believe it, still don't, and I didn't give a fuck. He was gonna get his ass whooped, and I was going to do it.

When he got to the back, I ran right at him. Paul E. saw me just in time and jumped on my back, and then everyone else piled on me. Pillman backed up and walked around me, and was told to get his ass out of there. Then I got in Paul E.'s face.

"Since you wouldn't let me get to him," I informed him, "you need to at least let me go out there and cut a promo."

"What are you going to say?" he asked.

"I'm going to say *whatever the fuck I want to say.*"

I went out there, grabbed a mic, and spent about twelve minutes going over every single detail about just why Brian Pillman was one of the biggest pieces of shit in the business. It was one of the longest promos of my career, one of the longest in wrestling history to that point, and I hadn't even had reason to believe I'd give it about five minutes when I started.

"You feel better now?" Paul E. asked hopefully when I got backstage.

"Yeah," I said, "but if I see Pillman, I'm gonna get him."

"Jack, I gave you that promo..." he began.

"If I see him, I'm gonna get him," I repeated. All through the rest of the show, all I was thinking about was getting my hands on that motherfucker.

After the show, I went looking for him. I found out that the ECW guys had checked him out of his hotel and put him in another one to hide him. I never got my hands on him; if he ever showed up for ECW again, people made sure I wasn't on the card. The next time I heard about him, it was that he was dead.

22

Title Shots

It might have been what the fans felt. It's certainly what the promoters felt. It's what everyone, probably including Mustafa, thought we wanted.

Big deal. A belt. Sarcasm at full volume.

It was more about winning by default. We were the top heels in the company, and had been for some time, with no one else hardly coming close. We were selling as many tickets and merchandise as anyone in the company. So why *wouldn't* we get the belts? Any promoter worth his salt would give people in such a position a run with them.

But those belts, which we'd get a few times, always meant about the same to me as they always would: not too much above jack shit. Of course I appreciated the fans calling the Gangstas the finest in the federation, and Paul E. for giving us even more respect, and the other teams that made us look great as we made it through 1996's last summer weeks at the Philly arena, but it wasn't too much more than just another match.

As long as the fans couldn't tell. At *The Doctor Is In* (a show dedicated to Steve "Dr. Death" Williams), a four-way elimination came down to us and the Eliminators. With Mustafa battered outside the ring, Perry Saturn and my future ally John Kronus set me up for their Double Elimination move.

Then I grabbed Saturn and planted him on the receiving end of his partner's high kick. With him out, Mustafa rolled back in and tuned Kronus up, soon powerslamming him almost through the mat. Moments later, I 187-ed him with the help of a steel chair. Our pinfall grabbed the biggest pop of the night, and Mustafa and I slumped back against the ropes like a lifelong dream had come true. That's how wrestlers need to come across when they first win a title.

After that, though, the only difference was that we had something extra to carry around. I still didn't need it. I was going to be over regardless. I think Mustafa (who took being the champion a little more seriously than I did) felt that, and he helped me show my decision with a little subtlety. He'd wear the belt upside down or backwards, and I'd throw it in a trashcan when we came to the ring. Guys from the streets don't worry about material rewards, and they sure as shit don't seek the approval of others, so the fans probably saw it as just another demonstration of the Gangstas' "Fuck authority and the establishment!" persona.

But there was more to it than they could see, or know of until now. It pissed Paul E. off like you wouldn't believe, thinking we were disrespecting the company by tossing the belts around. That was never our intent, at least not our first priority, but we couldn't pretend to be people we weren't. Being the champ was never a big deal for me, and if I'd gone out there and fawned over the belt and acted like it was some huge deal, it wouldn't have rung true. I couldn't have pulled it off; not because I'm a poor actor, but because it was just too fake.

To this day, the world title I got in Georgia just a few months into my career is the only singles title I've ever had—a situation I don't expect to change—and it wasn't on my waist for long. Later in my ECW exploits, when I started competing more in singles, fans were buzzing all the time about me not getting more title shots. I don't know if I was ever over enough in that area to be seen as a legit contender to the top strap, but by then, I think the main men behind the scenes had gotten the message that I wasn't going to be the type of world champion they wanted representing ECW.

Just one more part of New Jack's world that I don't regret.

23

Pay-per-view Approaches

The meetings were some of the most important parts of the show. They were also some of the shortest.

Basically, we'd all be in a big room together, and Paul E. would walk in and spurt out some formulaic version of "Here's who's working with who tonight, so you guys take care of each other, and have a great match!" We'd work out what details needed to be worked out, and then go about our other preparatory work, which usually revolved around finding certain substances to take away the pain and speed up the volume of the matches.

That was usually the case. But not always. In the fall of 1996, we got some of the biggest news in ECW history.

But we'll get to that in a moment. One of the Gangstas' most memorable ECW moments had come at such an assembly not long before.

Paul E. had walked in and met a verbal inquisition. People were pissing and moaning about the night's lineup. Everyone was whining that one guy couldn't have a good match with another, that this guy was going to make that guy look bad, that something needed to be changed to suit him, or him, or them. Sitting there chatting amongst each other, Mustafa and I just created a separate world for ourselves, ignoring the blathering. It would be up to us to close out the show, our violence and defiance of pain and death truly personifying the ECW spirit.

Paul E. stood up front, trying to get things organized. Trying to get people to listen.

Then he, per usual, decided to end things fast.

"Fuck it," he blared. He pointed straight at me. "You and Mustafa go first."

The room went dead silent. Mustafa and I fought off grins.

"How the fuck are we going to follow that?" someone blared.

"I don't know," Paul E. smartly smirked, "but if you want to complain about the lineup, I'll just let you follow New Jack!" Then he strolled out.

People wondered aloud how they were supposed to follow the guys who usually ended the night, how they could kick things up a notch from the guys who kicked hardest.

It wasn't our problem. We'd been told to go first, not to tone things down. And we didn't. We still came out there with our weapons. The Gangstas hit as hard, got hit as hard, and flew as high as we ever had or would that night. And the show played itself down all the way through the night. This was a teardown, not a buildup. The opposite of what a wrestling show should be.

We loved it, because we knew no one could follow us. The wrestlers probably didn't like it. Even the fans didn't like it. But Paul E. didn't care. One show's sacrifice was worth it to get everyone back on the same page, and for him to turn it.

And it worked. No one ever complained again.

The night in question, we'd have special reasons to feel the opposite. We were used to hearing Paul E. randomly erupt like a vocabulary volcano, but this night was something special.

Paul E. walked in, glowing like I'd never seen him. For a very long time, he'd been looking for a new way to elevate ECW to the big leagues, right up next to the WWF and WCW, and he'd finally found someone to say yes. For a guy who didn't celebrate Christmas, he was getting the biggest present of his life.

He'd gotten a deal to put us on pay-per-view. We'd be alongside *Starrcade*, *Wrestlemania*, *SummerSlam*, and whatever else.

That Christmas Eve, we'd be on the Sunday night show, and we, along with the fans, promoters, and everyone else in the wrestling world, would have a new reason to believe in us. We'd become *Barely Legal*. We couldn't believe it. We'd been in arenas and on TV, but pay-per-view's the dream of every wrestling promoter.

As the date grew closer, we all got ready. We were putting together something that even ECW fans had never seen before. On pay-per-view, you kick things up a notch, and we, as we always did in ECW, were going to go so much higher.

Then came two words that would live forever in wrestling history, for the wrong reasons: Mass Transit. The guy, and the incident, that would throw a huge roadblock right into ECW history.

And it was almost all my fault.

24

Mass Transit

The weekend before Thanksgiving 1996, Mustafa and I were getting some of our last warm-ups before the show, ready to square with D-Von Dudley and Axl Rotten. But when we got to Massachusetts's Wonderland Ballroom, we learned that Axl wasn't there. Family emergency or something.

OK, no big deal. Maybe we'd just do a handicap match with D-Von and let him kick our asses before taking him out. Or, even easier, just go to the ring, do a promo about what pussies D-Von and Axl were for not making it, and then head back and indulge in drugs and booze.

Didn't happen. I was in the locker room, dressing and bullshitting with the guys, when Paul E. came to me and mentioned he had a replacement. Some young-looking fat kid dressed in the stupidest goddamn bus driver outfit that didn't belong anywhere near ECW had gotten to Paul E., convinced him that A) he was 21, and B) he was a trained wrestler. Now Paul E. was saying I had to work with him.

I shrugged. I didn't give a fuck. I'd work with anyone. I've never complained about working with anyone—though not necessarily lying down for them.

The guy walked up to me.

"I'm Erich Kulas," he said. "I'm wrestling as Mass Transit with you."

I just nodded, like OK, whatever. He was just another opponent that I'd be too stoned and drunk to remember a few days later.

I wouldn't be so lucky. Neither would his ass.

"I got a couple of things I want to do," he said. "You're going over, but I want to put you through a table first, and then splash you on it. My dad's in the audience, and I want to impress him."

Excuse me? What the fuck? This guy's first night in the company, and he was telling *me* what we'd be doing? He expected me to help him look good, just so his dad could cheer for him? Was his dad going to buy out the next show, or get a million people to buy *Barely Legal*? You don't put on

98

a huge show to impress one person when so many more valuable people might be watching.

I was getting pissed. He'd walked into our locker room with a list of demands of shit to do to me. I was thinking about how many different ways I could kill this motherfucker.

Then he said the magic words.

"I never got color," he admitted, "but I want to get color. Could you do it for me?"

Oh yes. Yes I could. That was one favor I'd jump at.

I did a line of coke. I dropped a shot of vodka. I went to see Paul E.

"What I do to this kid," I vowed to him, "people are going to be talking about in ten years." In hindsight, that estimate was low.

Paul E. shrugged. "Do what you have to do." More magic words.

I didn't know Jack too good then. He said, "I'm going to get that motherfucker!" I didn't know he was going to scalp *the motherfucker!—Sandman*

We got in the ring, and Mustafa and I took D-Von out. Maybe this Transit clown was thinking that the spotlight would be on him, and he'd get to grab it.

Not quite. I smashed him in the back with a crutch. He got up, and I put him back down by putting a toaster nearly through his face.

He was still waiting for his payback. Still thinking he was going to get back up and whoop my ass. Never going to happen.

At this point, I think Mustafa was even confused. Things had just gotten started. I yanked Transit to a sitting position and reached into my pocket.

I pulled out a small knife. Actually, it wasn't a knife; it was a scalpel taped to a stick.

I stuck him a few times. Nothing really happened. But this guy had asked for color, and now he was gonna get it. I asked him if he was OK, like I gave a shit.

I gutted him across his forehead. Dug that blade right into his head, and yanked it right across. You want color, motherfucker, you're getting it.

He fell down, and blood was already flying out of his head like a balloon had burst. It got all over the ring, all over him, some on me. The tough guy was almost crying.

New Jack

People made it sound like New Jack just went out and intentionally butchered the guy. The kid lied about his age, lied about having a match before, and asked New Jack to cut him. It was just an unfortunate accident that he hit an artery. A lot of guys have done that when trying to get color themselves. Any time you go for color, you take a chance of that happening.—Fellow ECW star Jerry Lynn

His whiny dad was already in the audience, bawling and screaming for me to stop. Not what New Jack is about.

I climbed up to the top rope, held a chair in my right hand, and jumped down, slamming it across his forehead again. One of the biggest pops of the night.

It might have been the drugs and booze talking a bit, but at that moment, I didn't give a fuck if he died. This kid had wanted to stand out on the show. He did.

I remember looking at [Transit], and I said, "Is this guy a wrestler?" He didn't look like it. He wasn't in very good shape. I saw the blood, and I turned around and kept on fighting. But I did notice that the blood was gushing. When you get good at what you do, everything goes in slow motion. You can see the crowd react, and what they're doing. You see the referee, you see your opponent. But that night, things were a little foggy because of the partying.— Mustafa Saed

Paramedics came running into the ring, and I almost blasted them too. The microphone would have to be enough.

"I hope this fat piece of shit bleeds to fucking death," I roared at the audience, as many seemed to agree, "because I don't give a fuck. I'm the wrong nigga to fuck with."

Back in the locker room, it was just like any other post-match time for me. I didn't think I'd ever see the kid again, and I didn't care one way or another.

Then his dad came roaring in.

"What the fuck were you doing?" he yelled at me. "He's just a kid! He's only seventeen!" Ah, so the little shithead had lied to us about his age. Just one more reason to laugh Daddy Dickhead off.

"Fuck you," I said, laughing. "Get the fuck out of here." Then he said something that would set me home free later on.

Paul E. came running up to me.

"Get out of the building," he ordered. "Go check out of your hotel, call me, and tell me where you are. I'll rebook your flight. Go somewhere and lay low. Check into your hotel under someone else's name."

I'm in the match after that, so I try to go out there and bleed because there's some big heat on New Jack in the locker room. I went out there and tried to bleed to take the heat off of New Jack. I cut myself—multiple times. I wanted to go out there and bleed and show everyone that this is how it was.—Sandman

---

I went back to my hotel and used the name of the girl who'd brought me there. I flew out of Boston the next day, down to Atlanta. I was at the next ECW show.

All I knew then was that I'd kept my promise; people were talking about it, and they're still talking about it today.

But then shit started falling. Once word got out, we got kicked off the pay-per-view channel, and Paul E. had to beg, plead, kick, scream, do everything except literally kiss someone's ass to get it back. But as part of that agreement, he wasn't going to let me (or Mustafa) anywhere near the ring when *Barely Legal* finally took off from the ECW Arena the next April.

Only he neglected to tell me (he'd played it safe by having us lose the belts to the Eliminators in the first of the year). The show kicked off, and I was waiting backstage. All night, he kept going back and forth, saying, "I'll try to get you on the show." As the main event came in, I knew I wasn't going to debut on pay-per-view that night. It wasn't until the first *November to Remember* a few months later that extra-paying crowds would see me.

We all thought the Transit mess was over. Not quite. Three years later, I got hauled into court and charged with assault and battery. That was rich—ECW was full of guys smashing each other's heads in, hitting each other with everything we could find, throwing each other through tables, and they just *happened* to target me, for this? It was a bunch of bullshit.

I got made out to be a criminal that made Charles Manson look like a fucking choirboy. News nationwide blared about my "lengthy criminal record," calling me everything but a gang member (and they probably said that, without me even hearing it). They expected me to let the camera crews follow me home and find a stack of dismembered bodies.

I don't think anyone knew it would transpire at much as it did. People would bring all kinds of shit to shows, and he'd hit people with it, but most of the time that was a work. After it happened, the shit hit the fan.—Sandman

The Kulas family pissed and moaned about how innocent their son was, and how he'd just gotten caught up in something he didn't under-stand, just a helpless little angel attacked by the evil New Jack.

Then the jury heard the whole truth. That this kid had lied about his age. He'd never wrestled before, which he'd bullshitted about. And he'd all but begged me to cut him.

Then Paul E. got on the stand, and put things away for me.

"Did you hear (Kulas's father) call Mr. Young any names?" my attor-ney inquired.

"Yeah," Paul E. reluctantly replied (he'd been there for the dad's locker room rant).

"What did he say?"

"He called him ... the N-word," Paul E. said. "You know what it means."

"I need you to say it," my lawyer pressed. "For the record, you can say what the N-word is."

Paul E. looked at me. He mouthed the words, "Sorry, Jack." He looked at the lawyer.

"He called him a nigger," Paul E. said, his motormouth bravado gone.

I almost fell out of my chair laughing. I used that word all the time, like many black wrestlers do. I'd screamed it into a microphone a ton of times. What, did he think I was going to get offended by his explaining the mystery of "the N-word"? It's so stupid that people call it that. Just have the guts to speak your fucking mind.

I might not have been upset; I had tears in my eyes from trying not to laugh. But someone was: a small guy on the jury almost stood up and exploded. The only black man on a jury of six people, he was the only one who reacted.

At that point, I knew I was heading out. The prosecution took one more shot, offering me five years while the jury deliberated. But I trusted my intuition, my lawyer, and the effect Paul E.'s words had had on the juror.

The next day, I walked out a free man. Kulas was standing there, and I smiled and winked at him. A guy stuck a camera in my face.

"What are you going to do now?" he asked.

"I'm going to Disney World!" I blared. Not entirely true; I went out and drank with my attorney, and wrestled for ECW the next week. Soon, I threw the verdict right into everybody's face; I bragged about it on the air, wore a sign that said "Not guilty!" out to my matches (and even on a video game, it turned out).

The family didn't give in. They tried suing me. They tried suing Paul E. Nothing even made it to court. The kid's own bald-faced lies kept dooming them.

Even after his death. In May of 2003, a friend of mine called.

"Mass Transit died!" he roared. "Did you kill him?" He was probably kidding, but I don't think he'd have been surprised if I'd said yes.

Kulas had gastric bypass surgery to drop his weight, but apparently kept eating. Then his stomach burst apart and he died. His family still sued me, but that didn't work either.

People still ask me about this all the time, and my answer's always the same. I don't feel bad about anything. I don't think I ever did. He lied, he asked, he brought it on himself. Can't take responsibility for his mistakes. People just see what happened to him and feel sorry that a young kid got hurt, and eventually died, and they want a villain. They want a sacrificial lamb.

No, motherfucker—this nigga doesn't wear wool!

25

Mustafa Leaves

I couldn't believe he was pulling this shit.

Here we were, just having taken the titles from the Dudleys in July of 1998, and now I was going to be alone.

I wasn't scared or nervous. I knew I'd be safe; the fans would still chant for me, and I could more than hold my own in singles matches against anyone in the company.

I was just royally pissed off about the whole affair.

As we started defending the title against the Dudleys in Jersey, Mustafa missed a show, claiming he'd missed a flight. Whatever. It didn't bother me.

But something else did. The very next week, Terry Funk came up to me.

"I saw your partner last week in California," he reported. OK, that wasn't a surprise; Mustafa lived in the Golden State. What Terry said next, though, tossed an earthquake into my world.

"He was doing a show," he said, sounding very solemnly serious. "He came out with two guys, calling themselves the New Gangstas!"

What the fuck? First off, it was bullshit for anyone to just get up and go. But secondly, and more importantly, *I* was the Gangstas. More so than anyone else who'd ever been or ever would be. I could have teamed with anyone else (and I would do so soon) and have them get over by being an impromptu member of the Gangstas. When the Gangstas came to the ring, everyone was chanting for New Jack; it wouldn't be any different if anyone else walked out with me.

I felt like my time was about up, and I wanted to see what I could do with some other places. Paul Heyman was about to move on too. The business wasn't as lucrative in ECW as it had been in the past, so it was time to go.—Mustafa Saed

---

Like I said, I really didn't care if Mustafa had left. I wouldn't be happy, but the only real adjustment I'd have to make would be switching to singles pretty fast, and I wouldn't have an issue with that. It was more that his word was no good—not to me, not to the fans, not to the ECW crew, and, like I said, especially not to me. You don't just get right up and walk out on a company you've worked for forever, a big reason why anyone else knows enough about you to hire you away.

As Mustafa showed up next week, I went to Paul E. and handed him my belt. Here's one time in my career where not caring about being the champion was a huge asset.

"What are you doing?" he asked incredulously. He'd known about my aversion to championships, but this was taking it a little far.

"I'm not teaming with that motherfucker anymore." I told him the whole story. He told me not to worry.

"You put the belts on us," I reminded him. "Just take them off."

Even before he could do that, however, we sat back down, this time with Mustafa there. I informed Paul E. that either Mustafa was leaving, or that I was.

"No, Jack, let me explain," Mustafa began. "We were going to bring you in...."

"Bring *me* in?" I retorted. "*I* created the Gangstas! You were in WCW doing jobs every morning. For you to get comfortable enough to tell me you're going to bring me in on a tag team you created called the New Gangstas, you got me fucked up! I'm not tagging with you no more."

We dropped the belts, and Paul E. decided to go with the guy who'd worked like crazy for him since my arrival. I volunteered to tell Mustafa.

"They don't want you to come back," I told him. "I can't work with you no more. Our deal is done." He was gone, and I was out with other partners and opponents in about five seconds.

I was obligated to Jack to let them know I was leaving, but I didn't feel I was obligated to ECW. This wasn't a regular nine-to-five when you have to give a two-week notice. I gave a two-second notice, and then I got up out of there.—Mustafa Saed

---

I didn't miss a beat. I was teaming with Balls Mahoney one show and fighting him the next. He was always one of my favorite opponents, and I really wish he was still around to lock up with. I was at it with Justin Credible, Spike Dudley, everyone.

Paul E. came up to me one day. "You mind working with John Kronus?" he asked. Of course not. I knew Kronus could work. I felt that he'd been the standout of the Eliminators, as I'd been the standout of the Gangstas. His partner Perry Saturn had just left for WCW, and I think WCW wanted to bring both of them, but Saturn hadn't wanted that.

We jumped right into things. Early on, he and I were teaming against Balls and Axl one night in Pittsburgh. Before the match, we'd made a bet to see who could lose the most plasma.

Axl was the first to blade himself, and blood was all over his scalp, his blond hair really helping it stand out. Then Balls drew blood, and he out-bled his partner.

My turn. Inconspicuously as possible, I drew the blade across my forehead, itself both toughened and weakened by my previous slices. I saw a little plasma, more than most people would have liked to let go, but not enough for me.

I went at my forehead like a horror movie slasher. I must have raked that knife across my head a million times. Soon I looked like a vampire's wet dream. Smiling on the inside, I silently dared Kronus to outdo that.

He did. By the time he got done with himself, he looked like someone had poured a bucket of red paint on his head. If he didn't open his eyes, you couldn't see them at all. He won the bet.

I guess in hindsight, that seems pretty stupid. With all the diseases and shit going around, it would have been pretty easy for us to catch something, everyone bleeding all over the place and then getting slammed into the fluid. Not just the ones in that match, but those who'd opened the show. With all the bleeding, along with the drugging and screwing going on outside the ring, we could have picked up something a hell of a lot worse than a body slam, and then passed it around. It's a bit of a miracle that we didn't.

As he and I worked our magic at a TV taping once, Joey Styles tried to tie us together.

"New Jack and Kronus teaming?" he rhetorically asked. "The Gangsta-Nators!" I'm pretty sure that was meant to be a one-off one-liner, but people started taking to it and calling us that, and eventually it's how we became known.

I was always like, "No!" I didn't like it. But it was funny.

We took another title from the Dudleys, then handed it to the Full-Blooded Italians a few weeks later. It became the beginning of the end for the Gangstanators, as I started spending more time teaming with Spike Dudley.

It was right around this time that I had a chance to go to the then–WWF. They'd been discussing things with my agent, and I had an offer.

Just not much of one. First of all, they'd just created the Nation of Domination, and while it would eventually start the Rock on his explosion to superstardom, I felt it was just a rip-off of the Gangstas. I'd created that, I'd created New Jack—the character, the gimmick, the whole nine yards—and now they wanted me to be a secondary part of my own team. They had D-Lo there as a backup, with Ron Simmons as the head guy, and I didn't want to do that.

It wouldn't be the last time the WWF/E jerked me around. The very next year, however, it became WCW's turn.

26

WCW/WWE

I'm not entirely sure who in WCW felt like a bunch of hip-hopping rappers would get cheered in a company based mainly in the south (especially with a country band stable on the other side), but everything's a good idea in theory.

That, and the obscene amounts of money the company was paying Master P and his group of No Limit Soldiers to come to town in the summer of 1999, meant that the place had to at least *try* to get something out of the deal.

If the riches spent on nothing but hope and potential weren't a bad sign for the angle, filling the soldier stable with guys no one had ever seen before didn't help matters much. The company tried to Band-Aid the wound by adding Brad Armstrong to the group, but as great as he was, one known name wasn't going to save the situation.

When P and some others were about to show up with their "Hootie Hoo!" bellowing for a few months, someone on the booking committee had the brilliant idea to add a new member. A guy who was A) black, probably a strong sign for a rap group, B) known to audiences, audiences who'd been impressed by his ring work for years, and C) a pretty good talker that could add an ad-lib when fans weren't in the mood for rapping.

Sounds a bit like New Jack could have helped show just how limitless the soldiers were, couldn't he? Apparently, some names in WCW thought so too. I might have been about *that* close to being the Master's first lieutenant.

But someone with the power to stop my push did it, and I'm one of many he's allegedly pulled this sort of shit on.

"Bringing New Jack in would be a bad idea, because he's trouble," future WWE Hall of Famer Kevin Nash apparently told his fellow WCW booking committee members. "I don't think we should take a chance on him. It might be a lawsuit." A sad example of the dangers of inmates running the asylum, the booking decisions made by this guy ended up being a huge reason that the company went down.

The saddest part is enough other people felt that he was believable enough to listen to. One person doesn't make, or at least enforce, that kind of decision on his own, without backing from his colleagues.

It's amazing how much he knew about me without a single meeting, a single conversation, any contact whatsoever. Just all personal feeling and lack of potential.

Then again, you look at the way that WCW basically destroyed Public Enemy and so many of my other co-workers, the way they had hardcore matches with guys who had taken chair shots and gotten smashed through tables now having to take bumps off getting hit by balloons and friggin' *blow-up dolls*, and so much of it was just making fun of what these guys had worked so hard for in ECW. Not heading to Nash's world was a hidden blessing.

He might have forgotten it right after the decision was made, assuming it was him that made it at all, but I didn't. A few years ago, I noticed him sitting at a convention table.

I strolled up behind him. Onlooking fans might have thought I was about to launch one of my should-have-been-patented New Jack attacks.

Nah. I just grabbed him around the neck.

He spun around and looked up at me.

"What's up, Kevin?" I asked, with no cares in the world

"New Jack!" he said. "I haven't seen you in a long time. How have you been doing?"

"Kevin, here's the funny part," I responded, still grinning. "We've never met. But I heard you've said some interesting shit about me."

His mouth, eyes, and facial expressions all said, "Shit..." Was I there to get revenge?

No. I just sat down nearby and looked at him. He looked at me. Then we both went on about our business.

A few years after ECW went under, the WWE decided to hold the *One Night Stand* reunion pay-per-view back at the old Hammerstein Ballroom in New York, which had seen so many legendary ECW battles. Personally, I think it would have meant more in Philadelphia, but whatever.

As soon as news started buzzing in early 2005, fans started rattling off dream matches they knew they'd see. Since 2001, many ECW folks hadn't worked outside of the indie federations, and those that had been lucky enough to make it to the WWE hadn't been able to go to the extreme. For the first time, fans knew they'd glimpse the way things once were, the same style that had made ECW such an integral part of the wrestling world.

Tommy Dreamer was putting it together, and he'd be pulling in as many colleagues as could participate, or so we hoped. Those that couldn't have an official match would be running in to help out their friends, and take or dish out some tough blows of their own.

So it's pretty clear that many of them expected, and probably just as many wanted, to see New Jack on the event. I hoped I'd get to give it to them.

> [One Night Only] *was a one-hundred-percent setup to fucking fail. They spent about ten cents on it. Nobody knew it was happening. It was a fuckjob on Paul E. But we ended up fucking killing it out there.—Sandman*

Paul E. called and told me it was happening. I was waiting for my show assignment. A match, a run-in, maybe a balcony dive into action, I knew I'd get to do *something*. How easy would it be to find a place on the show for me? I didn't have to be the center, even to cut one of my trademark promos—they'd helped me to the top before, so maybe they'd help me get signed by the WWE now. I still had it. I just wanted to be there.

So what would New Jack be there to do? If you saw or read about the show, you already know.

The night before the show, I got an e-mail from the WWE legal department. It said that, because of some unresolved legal issues I had in New York, they wouldn't be able to allow me on the show. But maybe, of course, I could come around in the future!

They were bullshitting me. I had *no* legal issues in New York, nothing to resolve. They were blowing smoke and hoping I'd be too mentally blind to see through it. I didn't get on the show because certain people, probably very few people, didn't want me on the show, not because of any legal garbage.

I didn't even watch the show. It might have just been too depressing to see the next chapter of my homeland written with my assistance, but there was no way in hell I was going to pay to see my old team.

> *There was no fucking chance that New Jack was going to be on that show. It was obvious to me that they were never going to use him. He should have been there; he was one of us. He should have been able to run in with his shopping cart and do all kinds of shit.—Sandman*

Whoever saw the show, behind the scenes or in front of them, must have liked it. The show came back to Hammerstein every year until 2009, when they switched its title to *Extreme Rules*. Still, maybe the WWE was a company of its word. Because in 2007, my agent got a call saying they might want to try me out.

They flew me down to Fort Lauderdale, rented me a car, and sent me to the building. As soon as I arrived, I saw a familiar, though not necessarily welcome, face.

"Whatever you do," Dean Malenko told me, "*don't speak to Vince.*" I wasn't sure how to react. Was he messing with me? Vince was giving me a tryout, and his company had just paid for me to make it to the show. Vince McMahon isn't a man who wastes time or money, so why wouldn't I speak to him, if he might just offer me a job? If someone just walked by me and didn't acknowledge me, just to say hello, I'd be ticked, so why would this man want to be ignored?

So when the boss walked by, I disobeyed Dean.

"Thanks for giving me a chance," I told Vince warmly, looking him in the eye. He was very nice about it, smiling and nodding.

I went out to the ring, discussed the night with the guy I'd be working with, and returned. In all that time, mere minutes, my name had been removed from the night's lineup.

OK, something was wrong here. Johnny Ace, who helped run talent relations, stopped by, and I asked him what had happened.

"They switched some things around," he explained, "but you can pick up your pay."

"So I'm not working tonight?" I asked.

"No. But you can go and pick up your pay."

I did. No sense sticking around, and certainly no reason to sit there and beg for work. I hadn't even gotten to do my thing in, and probably around, the ring, and now they were telling me I wasn't going to show off my work rate.

"You got me again, didn't you?" I sighed. "You got me again."

To this day, I'm not sure what I did wrong, if anything. Maybe it was because I talked to Vince, or squeezed his hand too hard when I met him. Maybe I'd stepped in front of him on the way into the building. Or maybe he didn't know about it at all, and maybe he wasn't involved in my lack of participation to begin with. He might never have heard of me before that night, or thought of me ever again a few seconds after we met. Maybe anything.

While we're talking about the WWE, check this last piece out. People like to ask me, out of everyone who's ever been in wrestling, who I have would have most liked to work with if I could have. My answer usually surprises them.

Like me, his mouth got him over as much and maybe more than his muscles, and he never needed a title to get himself over. Like me, he could bring the crowd into the palm of his hand and farther into the match than about anyone wrestling's ever seen, and without rehearsing at all. Unlike me, he was great at cutting promos without throwing five or six four-letter words into every other sentence.

I'm talking about Rowdy Roddy Piper. If you say you saw that one coming, I'm not buying it.

Piper was extreme before extreme came about. Without weapons or blood, he always did all kinds of crazy shit in the ring, and he would take on anybody. If ECW had been around in the early 1980s, I bet he'd have been at its forefront.

How would *that* have been for a dream match? How would anyone have hyped it? "A Meeting of the Mouths"? Maybe we'd have a promo contest first, then hit the ring for part two. He'd probably be introduced first, tell everyone what he thought of them and what he was going to do to me, and then just sit there and wait. I'd come out and hurl my trusty garbage can into the ring, and he'd probably just sit there and smirk.

Then we'd throw down. It could have worked, and you don't have to take my word for it.

The WWE was having a pay-per-view in Atlanta, and I was in town for the weekend, working a comedy club.

Roddy went on stage right before me. Then I came on and did my set to a building jammed with wrestling fans. That's a hell of a different promo-cutting experience than being in a ring, but it's fun as hell.

For the first, and, sadly, the only time, he and I were hanging afterward.

"Man," I told him, "I wish I'd have gotten to work a match with you."

He laughed. He glanced up at me.

"New Jack," said the Rowdy One, "I think it'd have been good."

What might and should have been.

You know, I've never been secretive or really ashamed of my drug issues. I tend not to see much as a big deal. I've found that the more we play down our own issues, the more others usually will as well. If you share your own faults and flaws, people who go looking for dirt on you—usually for the benefit of their own pointless websites or endless quest for importance—have much less to find.

But the next part of this piece was one of my hardest to put on paper. It was tough to even want remember enough to write about. I've mentioned it enough that I couldn't knock out this book without at least touching on it, but I certainly wasn't anxious to do so. We might not be too near the end of this piece, but the next chapter was one of the last I touched up.

It's the story of the time when I almost lost my ability to wrestle, write, or do anything else ever again. Many of my colleagues could handle anything in the ring—any bump, any foreign object, any clumsy opponent, and just get right back up and keep going. But this enemy won't job to you; it decides when or if you're going to finish the battle. Many people, many much stronger people than me, have lost this fight. Here's when I almost did as well.

27

Too Close to Death

Sitting at home that infamously memorable Friday night later in 1999, I was hurting. I'd just come from a tough match, and I had another one coming up the next week. Tried to rest off the pain, sleep it off, just decided maybe I shouldn't move for the next few days. Probably even avoid deep breaths.

No, that wasn't working. I was still hurting, still awake. May as well do what I always did when I needed to feel better by means far past any legal pharmaceutical quick fixes.

Deciding to become my own customer—sadly not for the first time—I laid out a few neat lines of my powdery best friend. I knew what I was doing here; I'd snort a bit, feel better, and hopefully still have some left over for my next necessary snorting, which would probably arrive at or before my next show.

Leaning over, I inhaled the healing process. One thing you've got to give cocaine: it makes you feel better—fast! All your pain goes away, your body goes almost superhuman, you get one *hell* of an adrenalin rush.

And, of course, your heart speeds up. That was nothing new. I just sat back and smiled, wishing that this feeling could last forever, albeit with a safer way to obtain it.

I sat there and waited. And waited. And waited. My heart speed was normal, but it usually slowed down before long. This time it didn't. Kept racing. Even felt like it was going faster. It had never gone this fast. I started getting scared. If it got too much faster, it might die off.

Then I started to feel something different, and even scarier. It was like my heart was skipping. High speed. Slowing down. Coming back even harder and faster. My entire body seemed like it was vibrating. Was this the start of the convulsions that signal the dreaded OD?

Maybe I'd taken too much. Maybe my body couldn't handle it. This isn't the kind of mistake that you get a do-over on. Was that my destiny? To keel over right here in my loneliness, not even sure if someone would find me until I'd rotted? So many other wrestlers have died from drug use (many since then, sadly, many I'd worked with), and now New Jack was going to be the next epitaph.

Not long before that, I'd been hanging out with some ECW friends when we'd run into Louie Spicoli trying to have his dinner. Normally I probably wouldn't have noticed, but like I said, he was "trying" to eat. He'd lift his food to his face, hit himself in the cheek, the forehead, almost getting himself in the eye. Not clowning around—Louie was friendly, but not a real joker.

We went over to him. "Louie," I asked, "what's wrong with you?"

I knew. I think we all knew. He'd had drug issues for a while, but he'd cleaned up. The drugs were back. Not street drugs, but the muscle relaxers he'd use to collapse into unconsciousness, a way to escape. He'd taken them too early that day. He'd taken too many for far too long.

In February 1998, he took too many for the last time, drinking wine, putting down pills, just too much of everything. A past returned and a future gone.

Now I was next. That's how it seemed. I started to panic. I somehow knew that if I didn't do something other than wait, I wouldn't get another chance.

Feeling like I had nowhere else to turn, I actually called my mother. She told me to go to the hospital. I could hardly stand, let alone drive, so I finally called 911.

Soon after, I was in the hospital. But I was hardly safe; they inserted a catheter, ran test after test after test, not really knowing what the fuck was happening. I stayed there all weekend, not knowing if I'd ever go home. Any moment, any second, my heart might just give up on me and that would be it. And from what I learned later, it may well have been.

He cleaned up his act after he basically died from recreational activities. They brought him back, and he cleaned up very fast after that.—Jerry Lynn

---

Finally, after the longest weekend of my life, the doctor walked in with a bit of direction.

"I think you have AFib," he told me. Atrial fibrillation is about the epitome of an irregular heartbeat, stopping the heart from correctly pumping blood. It makes it easier for a clot to break off and go elsewhere, which

115

means I, along with the other millions of people with this condition, am at a higher risk for a stroke and heart failure.

Basically, I'd snorted myself into a bad heart. I may have had AFib before this—it doesn't always show symptoms—but this was a hell of a way to find out for sure. I'd be on blood thinners for a long time, and I'd have further complications with this, which you'll read all about in a few chapters.

For all of that trouble, I did an ECW show the next weekend. But I started making some pretty strong changes. Mainly, cutting down on the drugs.

As much as I've talked about the drug scene in ECW, and probably will some more, it wasn't hard to avoid the nose candy. People didn't really pressure me to keep at it. I didn't go into detail as to why I wasn't doing it; I just said no. Maybe they thought I was having an early midlife crisis, or found some health craze or something. I didn't care what they thought, and they didn't give a damn themselves.

If I wasn't doing drugs, they could always find someone who was. If I wasn't giving away or selling drugs, they knew who else to ask. For at least the rest of my time in ECW, I was pretty clean, at least in that area.

I could lie right now, and you'd probably never know. I'd like to. I'd like to tell you that that event truly scared me straight. I could give you the whole song and dance about *never touching it again* and *always saying no, even when the urge and opportunity were right in front of me*! I could do all that, like so many others have.

But I won't. You aren't reading this book, and I didn't write it, to be a load of lies.

I stayed away from the coke for a long time. There were times when I almost punched myself for even considering it. I had flashbacks to the time I spent at home, wondering if my heart was going to fade out for the last time. Lying in the hospital, not knowing if even the doctors would figure out why the hell I felt like I was being forced to knock on death's door. Fate had almost snuck up and taken me out like a ring run-in from hell; why would I want to tempt it again?

I did.

I never went anywhere near the levels I'd been on before. I never smoked or snorted with any sort of regularity again.

But every once in a great while, I still did it. Can't say that I'll never do it again. I guess I just trust myself to know when enough's enough with the powder, that I won't make the same mistake twice with the overdoing. If you're reading this, it means that I'm doing OK with that.

28

Spike Dudley

People still wonder how my next tag team came about, and I love telling this story.

Teaming with Kronus had been basically a process of elimination sort of thing, and we'd made it work. Me, him, Paul E., and the fans turned the Gangsta-nators into something special very quickly. I'd been talking about how just about anyone I worked with, teammate or opponent, would get over, and I think Paul E. might have been trying to test that theory.

One day in Boston, he came to me and asked who I'd like to team with that night. Maybe he expected me to want to team with Tommy Dreamer. Or we could try to tie together two seriously different styles, like me with Yoshihiro Tajiri. Hell, I was used to being the smaller part of a partnership; how about joining forces with that giant amazon Nicole Bass? Christ, can you even imagine that?

I couldn't, not that I tried hard. I stood there, contemplating the question. Then I noticed a little fellow sweeping up the ring.

He was one of the tiniest guys in ECW—actually, in all of wrestling—but that hadn't stopped Spike Dudley. He'd already snared the nickname "Giant Killer" after toppling Bam Bam Bigelow, and I'd seen him come back from injuries that could, and had, put down guys thrice his size. Fans had responded; the guy was over. His fellow Dudleys (labeled "brothers" despite some noticeable differences in height and race) had turned on him, so it would make sense that he'd join with a fellow family enemy.

This could work.

"Why don't you let me and Spike tag?" I asked Paul E. It's tough to surprise him, but this put his jaw almost to his waist.

"Spike?" he blurted. "But he..."

"I bet it'll get over!" I plowed ahead. "We'll be the underdogs!"

He slumped and nodded, clearly not expecting this or believing much about what he was about to say. "All right, all right," he said. "We'll give it a try."

It didn't take long. That very night, I was teaming with someone else against Spike's bros, and they beat the hell out of me. Then his music hit. Spike roared to the ring, whaled his family members, and we were off.

Unfortunately, this wouldn't last too long. We didn't even get to be awarded a catchy name this time! What was it going to be? The Dudstas? The Gangleys? Those things would have been too crazy for fans to chant.

Nobody's fault; Spike's a tough guy, and a hell of a guy outside the ring. He was hurt sometimes, or I was hurt sometimes, or the fans just felt we were too far apart and too hastily assembled to take too seriously. I'm still glad this was a part of my career.

As 1999 really got rolling, I had one of the biggest surprises of my career, as shocking to me as it was to the fans.

My past came back. But I kicked its ass.

29

Mustafa's Return

We knew that it would draw a lot of money and people. It was hot. Nobody could duplicate what we were doing. It was all business, and we were having fun when we were against each other. When we got back together, it was like we'd never missed a step.—Mustafa

The shit that Mustafa had pulled when we broke up, I was still bitter about it. I probably always will be, but it's not worth worrying about. I just have to remind myself of that sometimes.

When Paul E. came up to me that day in early 1999, though, I was as pissed as I'd been when my old partner walked out on me and ECW a year and a half sooner. I'd done a thing or ten since then, but I was about to be reminded of some serious shit.

"If Mustafa comes back...," he began. I already didn't want to hear the end of this.

"Will you work with him?" Paul E. finished. What did he expect? Did he think that I secretly had a twin, and that he was talking to the newer, daintier version of New Jack, one who just couldn't wait to do some ass-kissing and placating?

Hell fucking no, I wouldn't! I'd never do what Mustafa had done, and no one who I was working with would either. I hadn't needed his help to stay over, in singles or tags, so why would I act like everything was forgotten and jump at the chance to team with him again? Not me as a person. Sure as shit not New Jack as a character.

Yes, this was clearly what Paul E. had expected. So he went into the salesman mode that had put so many under his spell in the past.

"It'll draw, Jack," he kept saying. "It'll be good, and you'll go over."

I'd end up having to hear that several more times, and many different versions thereof. But the key words ended up convincing me to go ahead and put some dirt around the hatchet—that I'd be standing at the final bell.

119

I've laid down and put over as many guys as anyone in the business, and I'd never bitched about doing a job for anyone since I'd walked into ECW, but sometimes your personal feelings get in the way of ring performance. That bothers some guys more than others, and some are really good at putting it aside. I've talked about how I didn't need to win a belt to get over; hell, most of the time, I didn't even need to have a match, just a few minutes of microphone time. So getting over on somebody was never a huge issue for me, just like it usually wasn't for most people in ECW. That's changed a little today, but that's a story for a later chapter.

Here would be an exception. This is one of the few angles of my career that I wouldn't have taken the first step into if the ending wasn't already written in stone.

It went back to me being the guy that created the Gangstas. Mustafa's returning meant another payday for him, and I really didn't want to put money in his pocket.

But spend enough time with Paul E., and you'll probably end up ready to invest in invisible cars. I finally said fuck it and went in. He wasn't asking Mustafa and I to be pals, just to work together for a little while. We all knew that Mustafa wasn't going to be there very long.

I knew it would be fun, and real good, not just for us, but for the people, because it had never been done before. I had my other things I was doing, but that was one of the things I couldn't turn down. I didn't really care about [heat]. I didn't want to be there for too long, because I had some other places to go.—Mustafa Saed

---

In a move that really made New Jack the character look like a complete idiot, I "introduced" my old tag team partner at a pay-per-view that February. Anyone who's watched wrestling, for, I don't know, the past *century*, knows this cliché: the returnee's going to turn on the guy that trusted him! ECW was usually above recycling old bad ideas in the business, but this one was a problem.

Well, it was up to me to solve it. And it really wasn't that hard. Mustafa and I had worked together enough that we could pull this off on opposing sides. As usual, foreign objects were heavily involved.

We'd teased it for a month, but anyone familiar with our backstory knew that New Jack wasn't a guy that anyone wanted to piss off, and that he had so many more reasons to do everything but explode all over this guy that had put knives in his back both backstage and in the ring. When we landed in Asbury Park—spawning spot of two guys from the entertainment world named Springsteen and DeVito, along with a wrestler named Bigelow—he and I knew he was going to pay. To his credit, Mustafa went along with it all.

In the midst of the *Living Dangerously* crowd, I got him incapacitated enough to tie down to a table, and then headed up. Up the stairs, through the fans, all the way to the top of a nearby balcony. Much calmer than the thousands of screaming people around me, I waved at them, nodded, and took to the air.

Twenty feet and about a quarter-second later, I landed on him, my head almost driving right through his chest. We were both so fucked up that security almost carried the two of us back to the ring, and both of us took some good well-meaning whacks from our adorers along the way.

My entire lower body almost immobile and shaking in agony, I rolled over and held him down. Even in ECW, wrestlers didn't do this sort of thing just for a cool spot; if you were willing to go to these lengths, it was personal.

Even with all that, though, our spotlight got stolen when the Dudleys, by now his best pals, showed up and kicked the shit out of me. All just to let the fans know that our fight wasn't over.

That came about a few weeks later, back at the ECW Arena. Gotta hand it to Paul E. that he could help a guy get over without winning, and that's what happened here. Mustafa and his Dudley Do-Wrongs beat me, Axl, and Balls inside a cage (I didn't get pinned, which was important), but my buddies again planted Mustafa on a table in the middle of the ring, and again I soared off and landed hard all over him.

Mustafa was gone. As it turned out, so was I, but for a shorter time and more legitimate reason; I'd screwed my ankle in the match, and I'd be sidelined until the summer.

Was it worth it all? You better fucking believe it.

30

An Awesome Stapling

He'd just won the title, and no one, probably not even him, had seen it coming. This guy was one of the biggest in the business, came across like he could break boulders in half, and now was ready to run fucking rough-shod right over anyone who dared question his place at the top of ECW.

As luck, or Paul E.'s state of mind, would have had it, I was going to be this guy's first prey. Mike Awesome stormed right up to me, got right in my face, and let me know exactly what he thought of me and our up-coming battle.

"I'm scared, man," he admitted, his voice so far from this huge mon-ster that Paul E. was looking to turn into wrestling's next juggernaut, on the level of the Undertaker, Goldberg, or, in a few years, Brock Lesnar. "I'm nervous about getting those staples in my head."

I could hardly keep from laughing, but I allowed myself a smile. The staple gun had been a longtime ally of mine in the ring, and if there'd been a black belt for turning it into a weapon, I'd own it to the tenth degree. Match after match, I'd look like I was jamming staples into people's heads, hands, faces, everywhere. Sometimes my opponent would get it away from me and give me a taste of my own bloody medicine, me screaming and rolling around the mat in pain, looking like I'd just been mistaken for a stack of paper.

But what no one knew, and some will only be learning right now, is that I never had any staples in the gun. All an act. All selling between my opponent and I, and sometimes us trying not to laugh as the crowd cringed from pain we weren't feeling. Sometimes we'd hold things over our "wounds," making it look like someone had actually attached foreign objects to us.

Yeah, for a guy looking to make a brutal first impression on ECW doubters, looking to make New Jack his next entrée, Awesome didn't look much like the unstoppable type. And I was going to milk this one like New Jack always did. For a match taking place in a city nicknamed the Big

Easy, this would be one of his toughest nights.

It's a tough job being "fed" to a champion. You have to make them look good while still giving them a pretty good fight. If you let them walk right through you without doing anything back, your aura of toughness can vanish *real* fast. I was always known for being one of the federation's most extreme, so no one would believe it if New Jack turned into a jobber. That wouldn't just kill my career; it would have come across as so unrealistic that people wouldn't have taken Awesome as legitimately dangerous either. No one expected me to win, but I wasn't going to get shoved around.

Shit, the staple gun would be the least of his worries at first. I planted a

My infamous staple gun was never actually "loaded," but it sure scared the hell out of ECW's fans and my in-ring colleagues.

trash can lid upside his head, then the can itself. I put my teeth into his face in ways that Mike Tyson never dreamed of.

He recovered, punching the hell out of me and smashing me with a paddle. But he missed me off the ropes, and now I had him right where he'd been so scared to end up. I planted my staple gun right below his hairline, and pulled the trigger.

Awesome reeled back, grabbing his head, rolling around like it was the worst pain he'd ever felt. To this day, I'm not sure if he truly thought I'd pierced him, and his psyche was just fucking around with him.

Then I did it again, and by now he knew I'd played him. My weapon wasn't loaded, like it never was. He was still selling it like crazy, but inside, I know he was breathing one hell of a relieved sigh.

Either way, no one had ever manhandled the titlist like New Jack did. Maybe this would be the night that the original Gangsta took home the top gold.

Didn't happen. Awesome smashed me with a chair, slammed me out of the ring and through a table, and splashed me for the pin. But I knew that, as strongly as he'd won, the fans would be cheering as loud as ever the next time the fans heard New Jack's theme song.

Just a few weeks after my Awesome battle, it was time for my feud with the Baldies, the one that would change not only my career, but my entire life.

The staple gun got involved early; in a moment a hell of a lot more violent than most of the ones you'd see on most of our pay-per-views, with Angel pounding a staple straight through my eye at a TV taping!

Except he didn't. He was as good at faking the stapling as I was. I just got attended to by a bunch of pretend paramedics, went home, and laid around for a while.

Everyone felt great about this new battle, especially me. If no one got greedy in the ring, New Jack and the Baldies could keep the fans going— and tuning in and buying tickets—for a long time. There were four of them and one of me, although I'd get a partner here and there, and I was ready to fight through the entire crowd, more and more fans behind me every match. Angel had gotten the hardest blow, but I was sure I'd get the last one.

Then everything changed. You know where I'm going with this. The night that Vic Grimes and I finally fell, and almost for the last time. The thing that certainly no one wanted, or could have been ready for at all. The night that more than our ring battles almost ended.

But not yet. Before we talk about that, let's lighten the mood a bit with some of the few feel-good moments from New Jack's career! The ones that show that, although it's rarely seen, I actually do have a heart after all!

31

Some New Fans

One night, I believe sometime in the late summer of 1999, I was in the ring, celebrating my latest victory, listening to the crowd cheer for me and my music blaring. Moments from now, I'd be in one of two places: at the bar, drowning my pain in substances legal or otherwise, or relaxing in a hotel bed somewhere.

Then I noticed a small commotion outside. A fan had gotten a little too close to the action, and security looked like it was about to make him pay. As extreme and tough as the ECW crew is, you still need to be careful sometimes when fans are involved; a little liquid courage can put these guys (women usually aren't this stupid) in the mindset that they can kick your ass, or bring in weapons that even we don't allow. I've never had this problem with the fans, but too many of my colleagues have.

However, I didn't think that was the case here. This wasn't some drunken fool who just needed a good whack to knock him sober. It was a kid, probably a bit too young to really be watching ECW at all. He'd gotten too much into things, jerked away from his mom, and charged me.

The guards were about to eagerly take him down and out, but I stopped them. Every kid in a wrestling arena dreams of stepping into the ring, so why not? Why not just make it true for someone?

I did. Brought him into the ring, and he was already giving the Gangstas' hand-crossing sign. I gave him a high-five and escorted him out.

It was one of the biggest pops I'd heard. I'm not sure if it was sentiment, gratitude, or out-and-out shock. New Jack, a guy who'd bragged about almost killing a guy not long before, a fellow who'd knocked the brains out of one opponent after another, who'd started out as one of the most hated men in the business ... had a soft spot? That, of all the guys in the federation, the one guy who took time out for the youngest fans turned out to be New Jack? With other guys, it might not have been a surprise, or at least not as big of one. No one had seen this one coming.

It got over like crazy, and it kept doing so. After spending so long beating the hell out of another guy, and usually taking some serious punishment of my own, I'd find time to point out and bring in one of the youngest in attendance. Sometimes they'd go home with objects that had my or my opponents' blood on them.

Today, I still do it. Not every single time I'm in the ring, but sometimes I'll be in there, usually near the end of my night, and I'll let one kid get a little closer to the action. It's a great feeling knowing that, in a few minutes, you can do something at least one fan will probably never forget.

32

An Acting Career

Not too long after the Gangstas hit ECW and everyone in it so fucking hard, a fellow named Barry Blaustein got in touch with me. Like everyone else who gave ECW a chance, he'd gotten far into it. He'd become a strong New Jack fan.

Now he wanted to put me, and quite a few others in the business, on the big screen. This fellow was going to take wrestling fans farther *Beyond the Mat* than they'd ever been.

By this point, kayfabe was well on its way out of the wrestling business. The secretive nature that made wrestling so magical, almost sacred, was almost dead. Wrestling's a place where, for a few minutes, we make ourselves forget that we're just regular people, and become the people we are in the ring.

That's about gone from wrestling today. Many of us tried to prevent that, but ECW ended up becoming one of the main destroyers of the concept. Paul E. didn't know the meaning of subtlety, so I guess he figured that we'd just throw it out the door along with so many other things.

It became common for wrestlers to fight backstage, in full view of the TV audiences, and just *happen* to fall into a room where the heels and faces were eating together, hanging out, revealing what an act wrestling was. If Smoky Mountain had been old school wrestling, this was the newest.

So Blaustein figured it would be OK to reveal more of wrestling's backstage background than ever before. And he figured that someone from ECW would be a great place to start.

He showed backstage clips of the typical happenings of the then–WWF, and the real lives of Mick Foley, Terry Funk, and some others. The parts of Jake Roberts became some of the documentary's most well known, although I think that's due in part to people just wanting to see famous people suffering.

On the other side, there's a great shot of Paul E. giving his guys and

127

gals a pep talk before *Barely Legal*, letting them know where they are and what they're about to do. It's Paul E. at his most Paul E.–est.

I didn't expect this, and I'm sure Barry didn't either, but New Jack ended up becoming a pretty important part of the piece as well. He and I bonded in some weird sorts of ways.

I let it slip to him that, despite all my promo discussion of my hood experience, I'd never actually been to South Central Los Angeles. With the camera guy in the front seat, we hopped into his BMW and drove around doing some heavy photography.

There are also some things in that film that have been a bit of a burden to me since then (my "four justifiable homicides" might just have been a little dramatic creation), along with my acting career that didn't happen. I talked in that film about going into acting, and even did some script readings on camera. There's a really cute clip where one of the executives says something like, "Well, he's not Denzel, but he could be Denzel's brother!" I'll bet that's something they say to almost every young black actor who falls beneath the upper levels.

There's a pretty simple reason I didn't go farther into acting: I *sucked* at it. Well, actually, that might be a bit rough, but another issue was that acting's like wrestling in some tough ways. Namely, that you have to start at the bottom and work your way up, hoping for a break somewhere. That had been difficult enough in one business; I didn't want to start another.

My promos and ring world were enough to satisfy my acting desires. Then, I was sitting at home from ECW with a head injury when Paul E. called, asking if I wanted to go to New York. I asked why.

"To be on the Maury Povich show!" he responded.

"Hell yes, I'll do it!" I said. "Why am I going on there?" Nowadays, it seems like almost every episode of that show is men taking DNA tests to find out if they're a baby's daddy or people getting lie detector-tested to see if they know the meaning of the world faithful. Was I going on there for that? As I showed up at the studios, I still didn't know for sure.

Then they told me. It was a "Scared Straight" episode. They'd have kids who'd turned into damned fools out there, and expected me and some other people to go out and intimidate them into behaving.

What the hell? That wasn't my job; I don't ask other people to come raise my kids, so why should I get asked to fix someone else's? This would be a *hell* of a distance from my in-ring fan interactions. These kids wouldn't be wowed by meeting their wrestling hero; they'd probably just flick me off and walk away.

Anyway, I was sitting in the back, in the green room, watching the kids with their parents. We'd been told not to be *too* hard on these kids, but when I saw these little shits and heard their voices, my mind got made up fast.

These kids were throwing F-words at their own mothers, telling them to do all sorts of sick sexual shit to the teens, to each other, to everyone. I looked at them on the monitors, zeroing slam in.

"Oh yeah," I thought. "You just made this *really* easy."

I went out there, and, with as much intensity as I'd ever gathered up for a promo, got in these kids' faces in ways their parents would never have had the balls to do. No holds were barred here.

"You think you're bad?!" I sneered. "I'll take you out on 125th Street and sit you down for a few hours, and we'll see how bad you are! You're not bad; you're just stupid."

I thought I did an OK job being the first vertebrate these children had met in a long time. If their parents had any brass at all, I wouldn't have had to do this. I kept in the back of my mind that this had begun with them. I'm trying to remember that for my own kids.

If my work was the preliminaries, what happened outside the studio was the main event. The kids spent half a day in jail, then went to the morgue. They watched an autopsy of a girl who had died in a shitty hotel bathtub from too much heroin.

When they came back on the show, it looked like at least *some* of them had maybe uncurled their lifestyle. I'll probably never know for sure. The kids were asking for my phone number, and I was like, "Nooooooooo!"

But I did give more than just a boot camp chat to the kids. One of them was in the eleventh grade at the time, and she loved this 14-carat gold chain I was wearing.

"If you graduate," I finally acquiesced, "I'll give it to you." About a year later, she sent me a copy of her diploma, and I sent her the chain. Wherever she is, if anywhere, I hope she's doing OK.

Some of my most memorable performances, however, came in a very different medium. In late 1999, Paul E. informed us that we were going to become characters on a video game. As long as I got a copy, I was good to go!

Until I saw the game. *Hardcore Revolution* had just about none of the magic of ECW, as well as some generic band to play our "intros." Few things have pissed me off more than my depiction in that game.

"Fuck you, fuck you, fuck you!" I informed Paul E. Then I threw the game at him.

The mistake was quickly remedied. Later, in 2000, *Anarchy Rules* showed up with a larger roster, more matches (even tables matches), and a special song for me that Bootsy Collins had written. I was also screaming "Not guilty!" in the game, left over from the Mass Transit fallout.

You never really realize just how much effort goes into making a video game until you're a part of it, and I got a rough taste there when I heard about *Backyard Wrestling 2* in 2004. Alongside Sandman, the Insane Clown Posse, and a ton of others, including Vic Fucking Grimes, I'd be back in the game. Looking over the lineup at the game company in San Francisco, I shook my head in amazement.

"Wow," I said jokingly to an employee. "There goes the neighborhood!" It eventually became the title of the game, so it was only fitting that I was on the cover.

An employee handed me a script, and told me to read exactly what was on the paper.

"Say it like you really fucking mean it!" he ordered. I looked at my newest script.

Everyone else had lines to read for the game, but all I had to go was curse. "Fuck! Shit! Quit it, motherfucker!" If nothing else, I got to stay at a nice hotel in San Francisco.

Now it's time for things to get specific. Now it's time for things to get ugly. You got a taste of Danbury back at the beginning, and now we're going to go even farther. Much deeper. Into a place I almost didn't come back from.

33

My Fall at Danbury

Working with the Baldies had always been a highlight reel for me, but I hadn't known Vic Grimes all that well. We'd brawled after some run-ins, but never worked a singles match together.

So for me to find out I'd have to work a scaffold fall into an interaction with a brand new opponent wasn't exactly the easiest assignment of my career. But I figured, what the hell, it's a fall and another match, and he's been working for a while, so no big deal.

Wrong. In a show called *Living Dangerously*, I almost ended up going to the other side.

In the midst of one of Connecticut's typical heavy March snow jobs in early 2000, I didn't even arrive until the fans were entering the O'Neill Center. I hurried in and found Vic.

"Did you check the scaffold out?" I demanded. "Is it safe? Is it going to hold both of us when we're up there?"

"Yeah, yeah," he assured me. "It was fine." Then we delved into particulars.

He wanted two tables. I just wanted one. If you hit the first table, you're liable to go in any direction. You don't always know where, whether it's through the second table, to the ground, landing wherever and however nature wants you to. You hit one, you're going straight to the floor. It's not a forgiving place to land, but you know ahead of time where you're going to drop.

He kept harping on two. For some reason, I went along with it.

In the last match before the main event started, we, per usual, beat each other with every foreign object a wrestler can make look good. Per usual, we spilled out into the audience. Like almost always, even at house shows and in front of tiny audiences, I climbed to a much higher level. Then he followed me up the ladder.

Stepping onto the scaffold, I could already feel it shaking. Maybe I was just on an uneven part. I stepped farther out, and the shaking got

131

worse. Then he arrived at the top, but was too fucking scared to do anything but crawl.

"I don't think it's going to hold us," he said softly, his voice as shaky as the surface.

"I thought you checked it out!" I told him, all in front of a crowd.

"I didn't."

He didn't. He had known that at least one of us was going off this scaffold to the ground, and he hadn't even bothered to climb up and step across it. I guess he figured I'd just go up there, jump off, recover, and finish the match.

Fucking great. Now we're in the middle of a pay-per-view, dozens of feet in the air, on a structure that could tip over or collapse in on itself any second now, with over five hundred pounds of grown men on top of it, and only tables and concrete there to break their fall.

Vic wanted to climb back down. Wasn't happening. This was ECW, on pay-per-view TV, in one of the biggest spots of the night. If we crawled back down, we'd look like cowards and expose the business. This was ECW, and I was New Jack, and wussing out wasn't allowed under any circumstances.

I grabbed him. "We going on three," I informed him. Not a request. Not a question. Exactly what was going to happen.

But even as we started to fall, he pulled back. I pulled forward, and then we went down.

I turned my head to help land right, hoping to fall backward when I hit the table and take the impact spread out across my entire back. I figured he'd land next to me, or maybe near my waist, enough to maybe take a powder, but not end things early.

How wrong I was. That guy had done a full flip, landed on me just as my feet hit the table, and smashed my fucking head right into the ground.

When Vic landed on Jack's head, I was about thirty feet away. It wasn't good. I could tell from the way they went off that something wasn't right.—Jerry Lynn

---

That clip's become one of the most infamous in wrestling history, and if you've seen it, you probably remember more about it than I do. I'm not sure if I'm glad that it was filmed at all. It was crazy. Crazy's an understatement for how I felt at that moment. As far as my consciousness would let me realize, I went from falling off a scaffold to fading in and out in a hospital bed.

There I was, lying on the floor, seizing up all over, right in the darkness. Some people, both the audience and the crew, probably thought I was just selling better than I ever had in my career, acting out the pain that a normal fellow would feel going through this. Maybe they thought I'd done it on purpose, that I was out to end my career on a crashing note. That would be fitting for ol' New Jack, wouldn't it?

Remember, it had been less than a year since Owen Hart had died in the middle of a pay-per-view, falling out of the ceiling in a horrible stunt gone wrong. Way too many people, both those in Kansas's Kemper Arena that night and watching from home, probably thought that had been a wrestling angle too. There I was, brain fluid rushing all over my cracked skull, my eyes forever damaged, unsure if I'd make it through the night, let alone walk or wrestle, and fans were cheering.

That's OK. Fans can't always tell the difference between guys who are acting hurt and guys who really are, and we don't expect them to. The problem comes when the crew and fellow wrestlers miss that sort of thing. It took far too long for me to be stretchered out of there and taken to the hospital, although I don't think a few minutes there would have made a difference.

By the time it came out just how badly hurt I'd been—physically as well as the suicidal issues—everybody went nuts. The fans, the wrestlers, everyone. As I finally took my first steps back toward the wrestling ring, I knew I had a lot of support from everywhere. People showed that they were willing to look past the stuff that New Jack did that might have pissed off or disgusted them and cheer for the guy behind him.

I started getting messages, calls, all sorts of things from people who let me know I mattered. Not only from those who wanted to see me get back in the ring, but those who truly cared how I was. I got tons of messages, with everything from "Glad you're OK, come back soon!" to "Dude, I don't care if you wrestle again. I just hope you're doing better soon!"

For years, I'd taken wrestling personally. Maybe a little *too* personally. You don't put yourself in the kind of positions I got into for something that doesn't mean it all to you. I'd almost given my life away to drugs, then to a wrestling show. But I still had it. That meant something to me. There was more that I needed to step up and accomplish. I'd put myself through things that other people hadn't come back from, and yet, there I still was.

New Jack was about ready to return. I knew I'd be back as rough as I'd ever been, with chair shots and balcony dives—not at first, but soon—because I didn't know anything else. I didn't trust myself to make it as a mat wrestler (maybe I should have given myself more credit there), and I felt that fans wouldn't accept a different, lighter version of New Jack (maybe I should have given them more credit there!). I was going to work myself up to as good as I could with a damaged skull and shitty eyes.

Because now I had a new reason to make things personal. Wrestlers are supposed to put their individual differences aside for the good of the show, for the good of the promotion. I'd always tried to do that in the past, and usually succeeded. Not this time. It wasn't going to be a case of instant gratification, but I can be patient once in a while.

A guy had almost destroyed my career and ended my life, through negligence at best, and hadn't even had the common decency to make a phone call about it. I couldn't know if he gave a shit at all. Grimes would be gone from ECW not long after our "incident," maybe because he was scared that some friends of mine might make him pay, but I knew I'd see him again soon.

34

Things Get Hotter

> *Paul went up to the XPW guys and said, "I understand you're on the front row, and I hope you enjoy the show, but please ... don't fuck with my show!"—The Blue Meanie*

I'd work for Rob Black and his Xtreme Pro Wrestling guys for reasons personal and professional later, but during ECW's last summer of existence, they made about the worst first impression in history.

I'd torn my ankle half to bits shortly before, probably from flying off another balcony, but one of wrestling's rules is that if you can move (fuck being able to walk!), you're working a pay-per-view, doing whatever the hell you can. A little way through *Heat Wave 2000* in Los Angeles, I wobbled out on crutches, only to have De Vito and Angel pound my face in and jam staples into my head.

I couldn't feel too bad, though; after seeing me for just a few minutes, and then watching me get my ass whooped, the fans still chanted for me, louder than when Chris Chetti and Nova got revenge on my muggers. But even with my ego growing by a few small degrees, everyone in ECW had noticed a couple of people from XPW sitting in the front row.

> *Rob Black had bought a bunch of front row seats. His mindset was, "ECW's coming into our territory." The majority of us were just young kids in the business; we were just going to go there and show our shirts, and that was going to be it.—Messiah*

What did they think, that we weren't going to notice? Were they there for an audition? Had Paul E. secretly stepped into a deal with Black to cross-promote or something without telling us (which I wouldn't really put past him)? They'd been spreading rumors all week, and the Internet

135

had been anxious to help, and, yes, we hadn't exactly discouraged them ourselves. Publicity is publicity.

No, we were going to err on the side of caution, and caution told us that they'd come to show us up. To disrupt our show and steal it, along with the publicity and our fans.

We weren't having that shit. You can't. No matter if the people with you in your federation are your best friends or worst enemies, you always have to be a team. Especially in a business as cutthroat as wrestling, where promoters steal each other's stars and laugh about it and the top stars leave in a moment for a better deal (I'm guilty!), you can't show any weakness when a competitor's involved. If anyone on the outside even thinks you're going to be easy to push around, literally or figuratively, you're dead before you can stand.

All night, wrestlers came back to the dressing room and talked about it. No one left, and most of us didn't even shower. If your enemy's in your backyard, you better be ready to hunt, and in wrestling, your enemy is anyone who isn't in your company.

> *Paul wanted to send them earlier, but I told them, "You guys cannot fucking go out yet!" It wasn't time yet. I was the ringleader. Those motherfuckers wanted blood. I was sizing up a situation. I don't remember if I was waiting for the finish of a match, but nobody was going through that curtain until I told them to.—Sandman*

We all told each other to get ready. I can't believe these guys thought we'd stand there and let them cross our lines, I'm sure they expected a fight, but shit was going to hit hard, and we'd be at the forefront.

Sitting in the back, even with my bum leg, I was ready. Even when I couldn't walk, I wasn't going to back down.

With our last match about to go, the whole backstage was crowded around the door. We were watching as close as anyone in the arena, but at someone else, and for a whole separate reason.

> *Before the show, the XPW guys had been made to turn their shirts inside out. As the main event got started, they turned their shirts back, and stood up and started chanting. Word spread to the back, and the locker room emptied.—The Blue Meanie*

Then the match was lit. One of them reached across the gates and did something to ECW diva Francine, and she went nuts. We followed. Security tried to get between them, but that wasn't enough. Suddenly, you had the entire locker room charging over to fight. Guys that had just been beating the shit out of each other a few minutes before were all there, ready to go. The fans were right behind us, screaming the name of our federation. It was one of the loudest noises of the night.

Not much happened at that moment, and I couldn't do much, not hardly able to move in such a cramped area. But we knew it wasn't over.

The XPW guys got taken outside the Grand Olympic Auditorium, probably congratulating themselves on disrupting our show, for just a few seconds. But even out there in the parking lot, far from the cameras, fans, websites, everything else, we were going to show them the true meaning of enemy territory.

They got out there, but we were there first. And we were up in numbers, almost twenty to six.

This wasn't going to be a workout. We kicked their asses.

> *We stand up, and security was right on us—one of them almost pulled me over the guardrail. Then they escorted us out. A guy had my hands behind my back, and suddenly, I get smacked right in the head. I turn around, and this drunk old guy is just yelling at me, "You motherfucker!" Then I saw that it was Paul Heyman.—Messiah*

Mickey Whipwreck, Kid Kash, even Paul were all out there, bashing the shit out of them. We hit wrestlers, we hit ring crew, we hit anyone we didn't know. One of us would hold a guy down while many of us tried to paint the pavement with his brains. We had sticks, I had crutches, we hit them with anything we could find. I was bouncing on one leg and using the other to stomp on someone's face.

> *It was a one-way brawl, with the ECW guys totally engulfing the XPW guys. It was like the movie* Slapshot, *the final scene where everybody starts brawling. New Jack was on crutches, and he hit a guy with the crutch, then started spinning it around like a helicopter propeller, knocking people the hell out. They were messing with not only our show, but our livelihood. You go into the lions' cage at the zoo, you're going to get attacked.—The Blue Meanie*

And as they ran away, jumped into a limo, and left, as we were congratulating each other, we realized that we'd had an audience after all. We saw a group of cops standing right there. They could have pulled out the badges, the bullets, the cuffs, the tasers, anything else, and probably justified it with their protocol.

But they didn't. They were watching, some were laughing, and trying not to cheer. Cops on the job aren't allowed to show much emotion, but we got the feeling that they wanted to. They'd thought it was part of the show, just a bunch of wrestlers working everyone for publicity. It's probably one of the only times in history that cops intentionally didn't step in and try to end a gang fight. As a black man, I got a certain sense of pride knowing that a cop had watching and cheered while I'd beaten the hell out of some white guys.

When I look back on it now, I was just completely stupid. If I could, I'd apologize to Tommy Dreamer and Paul Heyman myself. We were just a bunch of eager kids, excited to be in the business, trying to please the guy we were working for. The ECW guys were drinking the Kool-Aid from Paul Heyman, and we were drinking the Kool-Aid from Rob Black.—Messiah

---

See, as I've said before, and as I saw many times, the locker room brotherhood of ECW was about the strongest I've ever seen. We had issues with each other, but, shit, you're around the same people, that close together, for so long, you can't avoid that all the time, or even most of the time. But man, if some outsider ever fucked with one of our guys, they'd end up sorry. Personal stuff got fired by the wayside for the time it took to destroy some rude motherfuckers who thought they could come from elsewhere and mess with us. Like with any team, if you have problems with your teammates, you throw them aside to kick the hell out of an enemy.

If you don't have that in a wrestling promotion, you're going to go under—fast. I've heard many people blame that as one reason that WCW went under: lack of teamwork. Too many people out for themselves. At ECW, it just wasn't a problem.

But some other things were. Things that we had no control over. Little things that got big fast and ended up ruining a lot of hopes many people had for the future, and a lot of things that many people had worked very hard for. As 2000 passed the halfway point, these things sadly became clear, very fast.

35

ECW Begins to End

Everybody in ECW was owed money, and nobody there had really made any money that they had hung on to. A lot of them had become acclimated to a very high-end lifestyle that involved an awful lot of drugs.—Bill Behrens

We all knew it was coming. We could see it, and I'm talking literally. People started whispering about it, talking about it, it was all wide-open fast. In a place like ECW where everyone knew your business, sometimes before you even did, secret is a foreign word.

By the time ECW went under in 2001, that was just the last shovel of dirt on the casket. The funeral and burial had kicked off months, maybe even a year, before.

We saw it in the locker rooms themselves. We were trying, working hard, doing the same thing we always had, but it all starts in the booking room. It's about putting together storylines, booking strong finishes, giving wrestlers some reasons to fight it out and giving fans some reasons to watch.

That just wasn't there. Not anymore. Paul E. was just too tired, too burned out, no creativity left. I can't say that our work was harder than his, or the other way around. As successful as we'd been in the past, it's hard to keep any wrestling promotion going for a long period of time. When you're doing as much work as Paul E. was, so much by himself, your tank is going to hit empty sooner or later.

Paul E. began to realize that they couldn't expand to other markets because people didn't want to put a show on with a lesbian kiss, bleeding in every match, wrestlers getting mock crucified, and on and on. He realized that he couldn't expand beyond the Philadelphia dates, because most of the tours [outside Philadelphia] had done OK, but not great.—Bill Behrens

Everyone had hailed ECW's TV deal on TNN in the fall of 1999 as some sort of great new beginning for the federation, that it was going to propel us straight to and hopefully past the national fanfare levels of WCW and the WWE. Then we found out the truth: that ECW was a giant guinea pig, just something that the network could test wrestling viewership with so it could hunt for the big bass of Vince McMahon Land later on.

TNN not only gave us a miser's budget for the show, they cut away everything that made us extreme. No blood, no "aggressive motions," like pantomimed stabbing, not even anyone getting hit in the head—nothing! How did they expect a federation built on pushing hell out of the envelope to pull back so quickly? Past that, what made them think that the fans who'd helped us shove that envelope would want to watch some Disney Channel version of our show?

They didn't. It's a common refrain among ECW alumni that we were simply set up to fail, that they only put us there to see if people would watch at all, so TNN could eventually go after the WWF. They did, and, for a few years, even snared it.

When Paul E. found out that his project had been sent on an un-knowing kamikaze mission, he started trying to get kicked off, hoping he could land somewhere else before all the money ran out. That meant more of one of his most extreme stars.

While I'd been all but kidnapped from TV at the start of the deal, now I was everywhere. Violence, blood, everything the rulemakers wanted now broken. When ECW eventually did get dropped in October 2000, you wouldn't believe how many people tried to blame New Jack. Look—I didn't edit the shit; Paul E. did.

[The TV show] became a double-edged sword, because the network immediately censored the product, and it had to be more about the story, promos, and workrate. The stuff that Jack was known for could no longer be featured. The thing that brought them to the party was no longer what they could do. Then the money dried up. Guys were showing up to shows, being promised money that never came.—Bill Behrens

---

By that point, everyone knew that Paul E. was just throwing shit to-gether and walking away. There were rumors that he was already working with Vince McMahon (probably true) or that Vince had already bought out ECW (not true yet, but it happened eventually). Once he got a deal with Vince, he didn't give a fuck about anyone else. The shows that he was booking didn't make hardly any sense at all.

Things like that bled over onto the workers. If your boss can't find enough reasons to care about his own business, you're going to stop soon. The ECW crew found that out the saddest way in 2001 as ECW limped toward its own farewell.

Well, I think they did. I was already gone, and it was for reasons far past professional.

I'd had my last real program in late 2000, suddenly the top contender for Rhyno's TV title. That was cool; I'd never worked with Rhyno before, and he was always a good guy backstage, so I thought I'd enjoy it. I did, so I didn't mind my company pay-per-view farewell being a loss to him at *November to Remember*. Then everything hit the brakes hard.

With a few weeks left in 2000, I was on my way to a show in Queens, and stopped to grab up my paycheck. Then my phone rang.

"Where are you?" Paul E. asked, sounding worried. I wasn't used to hearing him talk like that, but I had a feeling this conversation would continue with things I didn't want to hear. I told him I was in Manhattan, on my way to perform.

"Don't come to the building," he warned. "We got a problem."

Like what? Was there a health code violation or something? Was my opponent for the night (I really wish I could remember who it was) refusing to work with me, and, if so, was Paul E. taking his side?

"We'll try to get it worked out," he assured me. Then he hung up.

I waited a while, but that's not what I do. I called him back, and all but demanded he give me more than just partial truth.

"One of the security guys is here, and he's pissed at you," he explained. "He's saying you hit on his teenage daughter last week at the show in Manhattan."

What the fuck? Never happened. I knew it never happened. I hadn't hit on *any* girls at that show, let alone any teenagers, let alone one who was related to a guy I'd worked with for years!

I wasn't close friends with the guy, we didn't socialize much, but we talked sometimes. We'd never had a problem. And strangely enough, in the almost two years I'd known him, he'd never even mentioned his daughter. Never. That's something you'd expect a guy to bring up at least once, right? Certainly she'd done something by then that would make him proud to be her dad, wouldn't she? But I'd never heard her name or anything about her come out of his mouth.

This shit was going to get straightened out real fast, my way. Paul E. owed me some serious money, and no one picks my pocket without getting picked off. I hopped straight into that car and drove to Queens like I was in an auto race. If someone was spreading false rumors about me, they'd be quickly corrected as well.

Pulling into the parking lot, I called Paul E. from my car, ready to let him know I was declining his invitation not to attend.

Then I glanced up for a minute, and did a double-take. Walking right in front of my car was none other than the security guard who'd been looking to hand me a little police brutality!

OK, we were going to have this out right here and now. If he'd had a problem behind my back, now was his chance to elaborate to my face. I hadn't given this guy one reason to have an issue with me, but if he'd created one, I could cure him of that notion *very* quickly.

I stepped out of my car, ready to shake his hand, break his face, or anything that the situation could call for.

"Oh hey, New Jack," he said, glancing at me. "What's up?"

OK, maybe he was playing possum. He might have been trying to lull me off my guard and then ramrod through with the element of surprise. But he only *thought* he had it.

"Paul E. said that I hit on your daughter at the last show in New York," I explained. "You pissed at me?"

He gave me a look that I couldn't quite read offhand. Might have been confusion, might have been shock, might have been fury. I waited for him to move from word to action.

"Jack..." he said slowly. "I would be pissed if you hit on my daughter."

Yeah, he wanted a piece of me, and he was going to get more than—

"But the problem is, I don't *have* a daughter!"

Huh? Then he realized it before I did.

"Paul E.'s full of shit," he informed me, or, rather, reinforced to me.

I went into the building and hunted down my personal bullshitter.

"Jack," he said apprehensively, "what are you doing?"

"Paul E.," I said, much more apprehensively, "where's my fucking money?" He sighed. The plan hadn't worked.

"I'll go downstairs and get it from Debbie," he said. Debbie was the lady who collected the money from the ticket sales. He brought it back and handed it to me.

Thinking about this now, things could have very easily gotten out of hand over that kind of lie. I could have gone straight into tornado mode and started some serious shit with that security guy, who was being used himself. He could have gotten hurt badly, or I could have, and the other could have gotten into serious trouble. All because Paul E. didn't want to pay me some money he owed, and that he possessed all along. I'm betting he didn't exactly think that one through.

And he seriously underestimated me at the same time.

"You working tonight?" he asked.

"No," I said firmly. "I quit. This ship's about to go underwater anyway. Everybody can see it, the writings on the wall. I quit."

I walked out. After giving away six years of my life, half my eyesight, a shitload of money (not as much as I'd made, fortunately!), and everything else, my career at ECW was over after a lie and a walkout. Probably the most anti-climactic farewell in wrestling history.

Then again, it wouldn't be long before everyone else's company days would be over as well, without the first bit of fanfare.

I could tell ECW wasn't doing well, but I had a construction company in Salt Lake City, making all this money. Other guys were worried about where their next paycheck was coming from, but I was just along for the ride. [The last show, Pine Bluff, Arkansas, January 4, 2001], I remember being in the ring with everyone, but I had no idea I had just won the last-ever ECW match.—Sandman

---

It wasn't much longer until ECW was finished. Not with a bang, but with a whimper. I don't think the final show was even televised, let alone put on pay-per-view.

I almost felt bad about it, even tried to feel bad about it, but I never really could. I just had too many things going on, like working somewhere else and getting a paycheck. I'd already been lucky enough to find somewhere else, but a lot of my former crew wasn't, not for a while. I don't think any of them expected me to send out sympathy cards or make some touching, life-changing moments of farewell on the telephone one night. Just not Jerome's nature—sure as shit not New Jack's. If I'd played the sentimental act, they'd have seen through it like clean glass.

The WWE had ECW now, and it would be a while before they'd do much with it. I hoped they'd do something with me.

Even now, I'm not really sure what happened. But there's a ways before we get there.

36

My View of Paul E.

As much as I've mentioned Paul Heyman, or Paul E. Dangerously, or just Paul E., throughout this piece, I can't step away without a bit more on him. Not surprisingly, his people ignored my requests to include his words in this memoir, so I'm all that's left.

If Paul E. told me that the sun was going to rise tomorrow, I'd stay up all night to make sure. That's about how much the guy's words are worth.

Just about every time he opened his mouth during my entire ECW tenure, it was all lies whiter than the cleanest snow. Who was getting pushed, who was getting signed, how much we were getting paid, where the next show would be, deals he was making with this person or that company, every fucking thing you can think of and then more.

Here's an example. Like I said, we all knew that ECW was finished a long time before it was, but Paul E. either was well behind in his foresight, or, as we could tell, full of shit up to his enormous forehead.

"No, no," he said of his company's demise. "We're gonna be OK. I'm going out to California to sign a TV deal."

Yeah, right. Everyone knew what that meant. He might have been going out to the Golden State—though I wouldn't put it past him to spend the next week at home hiding under his bed!—but it sure as hell wasn't to do any deals, at least not for us.

No—it was to do that godawful *Rollerball* movie, which the few who saw it hated like hell anyway.

Funny story about that, though. Once, we were in Florida and he was babbling about how he was going to lead us to success and stardom, that all our problems would be gone soon.

"This ship is coming in!" he preached.

Then we found that even fate didn't believe this guy. We just happened to be on a canal, and a ship just *happened* to be passing by. I noticed it out the window, and got everyone's attention.

144

"Oh, look!" I called, hamming it all up like crazy. "There's the ship! The checks must be coming in!"

The room broke out in laughter. I glanced around, and saw everybody cracking up. People howled and handed me some high-fives.

But one person wasn't laughing at all. If he had the superhuman ability, Paul E. would have telekinetically torn me apart.

Even with all that, though, I'm really glad I got to work for Paul E. for so long. You can work with, and even work for, people for years without liking them as people, or even hardly knowing them at all. Paul E. wasn't the type of person I wanted to be pals with, but I didn't have to be. He may not have cared much for me as a person either, but he worked hard for me, as he did for most of his employees, at least for the first few years. As long as you could bump, as long as you could draw, and as long as you wouldn't whine about losing a match here or there, Paul E. didn't give a shit about being your best friend, worst enemy, or anything else in between.

To his credit, he always thanked me, along with everyone else, for our work on the shows. He paid me what he said; I was one guy lucky enough to not be owed money when ECW died.

I might have still been successful in the wrestling business if I'd never gone to ECW, but probably not. I don't have to worry about that now. Paul E. gave me a great chance (as did Tod Gordon, Al Snow, and others who got me started in the company), and I don't think I'd have been getting calls from everyone from TNA to CZW to every other federation I've worked for in the past two decades without Paul E.'s help. So, hey, Paul E.—thanks a lot!

You bald-faced liar.

37

XPW

After ECW went down, Paul E. told us all the same shit he'd blathered to get us into ECW and to keep us there as long as he had. We'd all get jobs with the WWE, we'd all make lots of money, he'd get Vince McMahon to push aside all the guys McMahon already had and make us into stars.

All his usual bullshit. I knew we'd be stuck in the indies or sitting at home, getting paid a little, if anything at all.

Yeah, some guys followed him to the WWE, with that invasion angle that everyone thought would blow open wrestling world-wide. Didn't happen—the people who actually "invaded," like our guys and the ones from WCW, got their asses kicked and were made to look like shit because the WWE didn't want to look bad at all. Even Paul E. got used for a while at first. They made him a heel announcer, then had him kiss up to Vince Mc-Mahon after the "invasion." He did a good job working with the creative part of the WWE, but it took another year, when they put him alongside Brock Lesner, to get anything going in the ring.

He called me once, asking if I'd like to cut a promo for the invasion. Problem was, it was going to be by satellite. While my partners in ECW would be on the show, in the ring, I'd be off in some station hundreds of miles away, yelling at a camera.

No way. If I couldn't be physically at the show, I didn't see any reason to be on it.

I was glad I didn't go. And the invasion wasn't the only reason. It was time for me to settle another score, one that the WWE would never have let me do right.

A little later in 2001, I got in touch with Kevin Kleinrock. We'd done some small projects together before, and he'd always been pretty straight up with me. Along with this porn producer named Rob Black, Kevin was in this venture called Xtreme Pro Wrestling, which basically took everything ECW did and kicked it up a few (thousand) notches.

Yes, I remembered Black very well. He remembered me. We met, we talked, we shook hands, we agreed. Nothing explosive. I met his guys, some of whom had participated in the beat-down of Los Angeles the summer before.

Did they think I was going to apologize or explain or show any kind of remorse? New Jack doesn't carry emotions like that. Kicking their asses had been the right thing at the right time. And after ECW, XPW seemed like a fitting place for a guy like New Jack to visit. People wouldn't be surprised to see me at a place like that, but I was betting they'd be glad.

There was one guy I was *very* pleased to see. I don't think he felt the same.

By the way, if I hadn't figured it all the way out by now, anyone who met him could tell early on what a prince Rob Black was. The guy had been in porn since the early 1990s, and made his own company called Extreme Associates, a pretty innocuous name for a company specializing in porn full of physical abuse and women puking in the middle of the act.

I can't say it was all bad, though—he let me go into his warehouse and look at all the porn he did. I'd load up boxes of the stuff and mail it back home. Then I'd sell it to porn shops and make some extra money.

If I'd listened to another offer of his, however, I might not be writing this right now.

Messiah was one of XPW's top wrestlers. He and I hadn't exactly had a great first encounter, as he'd been part of that one-night "invasion" brawl back at *Heat Wave 2000*, although he and I hadn't squared off that night. But he knew I was better to have as a friend than an enemy, so we got along pretty well when I first showed up in XPW.

We had no idea New Jack was coming in. At his first show, we're just in the ring, working out, and then suddenly, there's New Jack! He got in the ring and ran the ropes, and my first impression was, "Wow, he's a lot bigger *than I thought he was!" One thing that stands out about that night is that after the show, he cut a great, long promo about showing up in XPW and bringing a pack of ECW guys with him. He did it all in one take, and I was just blown away by it, because I'm a twenty-take guy!—Messiah*

Once I was working with Supreme against Messiah and Grimes in a tag match. It was basically your typical run-of-the-mill, double-tables-in-the-middle-of-the-ring, vertebrae-shatter-fest, but this time there would come a twist.

The tables would be set on fire.

Problem was, Messiah was biting the can of lighter fluid open, and ended up getting it all over his face, then on me! He also got too much on the tables. When the flames were finally lit, it didn't burn long enough, and fluid was still all over the tables.

That's why, when I got suplexed on top of them, I still had it all over my back. When I hit those tables, I about turned into a human fireball.

My shirt was absolutely engulfed in flames (fortunately, I had on an extra one—if I'd been doing my typical bare-shouldered act that night, my skin could have been blasted even blacker!). I rolled out of the ring and started running like I was on fast forward; there went that whole "stop, drop, and roll" shit right there! I bolted out of the ring and started running in circles, hauling around the corner of the ring and nearly smashing into Rob's girlfriend Lizzy Borden. As I tore off my shirt, I suddenly got blasted on just about every side by fire extinguishers. It wasn't until a few minutes later that everyone realized that Supreme had long since pinned Grimes to give us the match.

I thought Jack was legitimately going to kill me for that. But when I went to the back to see if he was OK, he looked up at me with a big smile. That was something I'll never forget. He was happy, I was happy. He can work and make it look like he's killing you, but he took care of me in the ring great.—Messiah

---

During my XPW time, Rob heard that the Messiah was messing with Lizzy, who'd been right next to him in the X-ratings. I didn't pay much attention to it; true or not (and I have no idea there), it had nothing to do with me.

In August 2002 (Messiah had left the company by then), two guys broke into his house with some garden shears and left with his left thumb. The guy was in his mid–20s, early in his career, and now he'd been put through an ordeal that would have put most guys out of the business for good.

It went all over the country, even getting on *America's Most Wanted*. They showed a bunch of clips of the wrestlers, especially me, with my face beaten in and all bloody. They may have just been pissed because I wouldn't go on their show, because they made me, and the business, look horrible.

Saddest thing is, even today, after all that, they've never caught the guys who did it (though I'm part of long list that's pretty sure Black was involved).

But I have to give Messiah credit where it's due—he was back wrestling just a few weeks after he got attacked (not for XPW, good Lord no!), and went at it for a few more years. Of course, prince that I am, I could never resist teasing him about not being able to jerk off anymore!

Jack used my injury in promos. Lots of guys teased me about it, but I didn't care. That's just locker room stuff. Jack had never called me before, but he called me the day after it happened to see if I was OK. That meant a lot. He did promos about me losing my thumb, but that was fine after he called me.—Messiah

---

Hell yeah, I called him. Why wouldn't I? The guy had just had his thumb cut off. I wasn't really trying to be nice. Who wouldn't just pick up the phone and give someone a call after something like that? I really hope the people who did it get caught someday. Nobody deserves that bullshit. I'm glad Messiah came back and made it in the business.

Having the attack was one of the best things that ever happened to me, because as a result, I met my wife and got my kids. I wouldn't change anything. My wife's boyfriend at the time was a promoter who wanted to use me, so that's how I met her. It sounds like a Hallmark card or a T-shirt to say it, but it was a good thing. Maybe one day, I'll have a nervous breakdown about it, but right now, I'm fine with it.—Messiah

---

Anyway, I spent the rest of 2001 and the first of 2002 working with everyone from Vampiro to the guys in the Insane Clown Posse, but I, along with all the other ECW stars there, knew that XPW was never going to be our old company. They had the same blood, thumbtacks, barbed wire, all kinds of hardcore shit, but it could never compare to ECW, which had guys that could actually wrestle. People took it *way* too far in XPW, and if New Jack is telling you that, it means something. Even Black took it too far, just like he did with every fucking thing, which is part of the reason why he and Lizzy ended up doing jail time for distributing their shit (can't hide that far under the First Amendment), something that ended up killing XPW for good in 2003.

> *XPW was a bad version of ECW. It was badly booked and badly run, and the owner should have been in jail. One day, Jack started a show doing armdrags and hiptosses, just because he knew no one would expect it. You go to a promotion where halfway through the show, everybody's going to be bleeding, so if you're on first, why bleed? If bleeding won't make you stand out, why bother?—Bill Behrens*

I was gone by then, but I never cared too much about what anyone else was up to, as long as my paychecks were getting signed and clearing. I took it in and sucked it all up.

Because I was about to get my final revenge on Vic Motherfucking Grimes.

38

Grimes Goes Down

XPW had people hitting each other with all kinds of shit, bleeding everywhere like you wouldn't believe. I started working with that SOB Grimes, and he shoved me through a table—on fire. The motherfucker's debts just kept growing.

People who knew I was already pissed at him might have thought I'd gotten revenge with a good table slam back at the Grand Olympic in May of 2001, but he fired my ass off the balcony of that same place the next January. They might have been lulled into thinking that Vic and I were cool, that we'd put everything aside for the bygones' behalf. He might have felt that way too. I went out of my way to make him feel that way, as far as I've ever gone for anyone.

Check this—early in 2002, I took the biggest bump of my career, before or since, just to lull him into a sense of security. From more than thirty feet in the air, I let him push me off, with me smashing through a table and landing right on my side on a hard wood floor. I got carried back to the dressing room, and Grimes came in to see me.

"Holy *shit*...," he whispered in amazement. I acted like I was in pain, which wasn't all a put-on, but I was smiling inside. I guess he figured that if I was willing to bump that hard for him, I was going to go to any lengths to put him over. It's all about being a team player in wrestling, isn't it?

Even when we talked, I was standoffish, but friendly. I wanted him to believe that we wouldn't have any problems.

Wrong. All just one big fucking buildup. Everything just slipping right into place.

We were having a big show in Los Angeles on February 23, 2002. They were calling it *Freefall*. Doesn't take much to see where this one was headed.

Rob called us together and pulled out a quarter. He was going to flip it, and the winner *wouldn't* get thrown off a scaffold from forty feet in the air, crash down through a pile of tables, and land splat in the ring.

151

I laughed. "You can flip that motherfucking coin all day long!" I snorted. "Vic's going off that motherfucker!"

Rob and Vic laughed. I guess they figured it was only fair that Vic got some payback after Danbury, and everything else I'd pretended to do on his behalf since. Only I knew that his pay would be with heavy interest.

Still, I stayed professional. We talked about the match when I got to town the day before it happened, and the day it did. As I left my hotel for the Grand Olympic Auditorium that afternoon, I had my driver stop off at a pawnshop for a little ... assistant.

I did an 8-ball of cocaine, and the whole night I was buzzing like crazy. My fellow ECW alumnus the Sandman—who'd been friggin' wasted by WCW over his year, playing a pathetically beaten down version of his former self named Hardcore Hak—took the XPW Deathmatch title in the semi-main event, and now it was finally time for revenge.

He told me what he was going to do; I was his confidante in the locker room. We'd known each other for years, and I knew he was going to do that, but I couldn't believe it.—Sandman

---

I was out first, telling the fans, as only New Jack could, how much they meant to me, tossing in "motherfucker" and "goddamn" as many times as I could. Then I promised Vic that one of us wouldn't walk out tonight. He, and the fans, probably thought it was just another promo.

I wrapped a chain around his neck and broke some objects over his head. I carved him up with a fork and tore his forehead open with barbed wire. He sliced me open and smashed me in the head with some other weapons.

Finally, he pointed skyward. Then he started climbing up to the top. I did likewise.

Forty feet later, we were at the top. There were thousands of people in the stands making all kinds of noise, chanting my name, but I couldn't hear them. I'd waited too long for this moment, and nothing was going to stop me. If I'd looked around and seen just how goddamned far in the air we were, I might have lost my own nerve.

Still, I was throwing working punches. I wanted him to believe that everything was cool.

We went back and forth on that scaffold for a while. Then I pulled out my secret weapon, the one I'd grabbed on the way to work that day.

A taser. Stone Cold Steve Austin had never given the type of stunning I was about to hand out to this guy. Shit was about to get very real.

I planted it into his side, his face, his neck, his chest, his stomach. Eight times I shocked him. He might have had a heart attack if I'd kept it up, but I didn't give a shit. This guy had almost ended my career and my life, and never bothered to call or check on me when I was out, so he meant as much to me as it looked I did to him.

Finally, I picked him up. It was time for me to keep the promise I'd made to the fans.

"Jack," he gasped, "I can't feel my legs!"

"Don't worry," I retaliated. "You ain't gonna need 'em!"

Then I threw him. There were stacks of tables on the mat that he thought would break his fall; I was trying to throw him past them. He hit a few, then landed on the ring ropes and fell back on the mat.

I stood on the scaffold, waving my arms, pounding my chest, roaring at the fans, who were still chanting my name.

Looking down at him, I loved it. I was hoping he was paralyzed. Turned out he'd "only" broken his femur.

> *Unfortunately, or fortunately, depending on whose point of view, Jack did one of the nicest things you can ever do when you're trying to hurt somebody badly, and that was that he tased [Vic] first. By tasing him, when Vic took the bump, bouncing off shit all the way down, he was knocked out. He was a ragdoll, and that saved his life. If Jack hadn't tased him, he might well have died. You have a tendency to stiffen up if you're aware of things, as opposed to relaxing. Pretty hard to relax if you're taking that bump.—Bill Behrens*

Eventually, I climbed down. Down to the ring and down to him.

"Now we're even, motherfucker," I assured him.

I was done. I walked out of there, got my money, went back to the hotel, and walked straight out of XPW.

> *That was the status quo. You learn to accept what happens. The rest of the world thought it was fucking crazy. They couldn't believe we just played it off, like that's the way it is. Dude, in wrestling sometimes, that's the way it is! So many wrestlers die—if you're going to die in wrestling, that's the way it is.—Sandman*

39

Gypsy Joe

I pulled into the parking lot of the TV studios in Columbia, Tennessee, ready for my next one-shot deal. I was going to show up, whoop some local guy, get paid, and keep moving forward.

A promoter had called me a few days before, asking if I'd show up in his land to cut a few promos before the match, letting everyone know they'd soon get a close-up, bloody look at New Jack. I was working with some guy named Gypsy Joe, who, said the promoters, knew the ins and outs of the business, definitely worth working with. Someone who could relate to my hardcore style as I beat hell out of him.

Two guys were standing outside the studio. One of them was bigger than me, and he certainly looked like he could go around and around in the ring. Maybe take a few chair shots and a splash, or maybe give a few and look good.

The other looked like his dad. Maybe here to cheer his son on. Hopefully, it wouldn't end up like the Mass Transit situation!

Assuming I'd be working with the guy within a decade of my age, I went up to the younger one, shook his hand, and introduced myself.

"Hi," he said. "I'm Hammerjack."

Ok, so maybe Joe was inside somewhere.

The great-grandpa-looking guy spoke up. "I'm Gypsy Joe."

I looked at him. I started laughing, expecting someone to come up behind me and yell, "Gotcha, new guy!"

He didn't laugh. I stopped.

Was he serious? I was going to work with this guy? I'd never heard of him, but I don't care if he'd been the greatest wrestler alive a few (dozen) generations before. This guy looked a hundred years old, and he didn't belong in the ring with *anyone*, let alone a hardcore match. It turned out that he'd actually *trained* Hammerjack.

I roared into the building and hunted down the promoter.

"This is only going to go one of two ways," I told him. "Either we're going to do a match, or a comedy match." I didn't do comedy matches, and this guy didn't need to be between the ropes.

"It'll be fine, Jack," he assured me. "This guy's been around a long time, and he knows his stuff in the ring. He can handle himself."

New Jack doesn't do comedy. I've been around it, and there's others who can do it well, but that's not been me, never has been nor will be. I've been asked to do it in just about every federation I've been a part of, even some of my one-shot deals, but I always say no. You can't threaten and insult people, go nuts with weapons, take a huge beating and then come back, and expect people to want to laugh at you, or to pay money to do so.

If I'd ever done any comedy, I'd be helping someone mock everything I worked for to become New Jack, and I'd be lowering myself. Anyone who knows me knows that I have a pretty good sense of humor, but even then, it's pretty focused, pretty specific. There aren't really *that* many things that make me laugh at all, and self-mockery in the ropes isn't going to be on that list.

We cut the promos. I told the truth. I wasn't going to take anything easy on this guy. I didn't really think about it too much. Many wrestlers might have been worried about how to work around this guy's weaknesses (that would take forever!) and still make him look good, but not me. I was going to do the same as I always did. I was diving off balconies and getting smashed through tables in front of a few hundred people at small shows, or in front of thousands in pay-per-views. When New Jack came out to wrestle, you always got the same guy—heel or face, tag team or singles, crowd of 10 or 10,000. I wasn't going to change now.

Me and Jack were hanging out a little bit. I walked in and saw him playing video games, my first impression was, "Be careful—this guy doesn't like white people!" I'd always heard that. But then I found out that Jack was just a real dude like the rest of us. Gypsy Joe had been a hardcore legend in Mexico, Japan, Korea, Puerto Rico, all over the world. Joe was cutting promos like, "I'm going to show New Jack who the hardcore legend is!" I'd seen Joe do some crazy shit, so I thought he'd be OK. We all thought they'd take care of each other.—Hammerjack

---

The night of the show, Joe came up to me.

"Listen, kid," he promised. "I can teach you a lot. Just listen to me."

The crazy thing is, I think he might have meant what he was saying. He thought I was there to listen and learn. I'd been in the business for over a decade, and now I was going to learn from a guy who should have quit before I'd ever began?

Up until the moment the ring announcer called our names, I still thought that this might be a rib. Maybe I'd get in the ring and Joe would blare something like, "I was going to fight you, Jack, but my arthritis is kicking up too hard, so I've got *this guy* as a sub." The other guy would come out, I'd look surprised, and we'd have a match. That, I could pull off.

Heading out to the ring, I still wasn't really worried. This guy knew what he was getting into with me, and now he, and the (admittedly few!) fans in attendance would find out.

I kept walking—and then I heard the same kind of shit I'd thought I'd left behind when I said goodbye to Smoky Mountain.

"Hey, nigger! Go back to Africa!" roared the crowd (Columbia's just about thirty miles from Pulaski, where the Ku Klux Klan was first formed). "Get out of here, nigger!" Joe himself wasn't saying that shit, but he was in the position where I'd have to make him pay. I felt like I had been brought to the lion's den, and now I was going to kill this old motherfucker.

We locked up, and I pushed him against the ropes. Then I smashed him twice in the head. Already, people were whining about me not taking it easy on the old guy.

He started no-selling me. I was laying it in, and he didn't show it at all. Nobody fucking does that to me. Then he head-butted me in my nose.

That's when shit got real. I threw him into the ropes—as if he could run—and chopped him down. Some objects were in the ring, and I started hitting him with them. I picked him up like I was going to body-slam him, and threw him out of the ring. He held the ropes on his way over, and didn't even leave his feet.

He kept no-selling, and we walked around the ring. Eventually I lost it, threw him on the ground, and started choking him with a chain. By now, people were leaving their seats in fear, disgust, whatever. Shows like this one typically stick to the traditional route in wrestling, but they knew they weren't getting that when they asked me to show up.

Jack was working with him, and Gypsy was no-selling what Jack was doing. Jack figured, "OK, if you're not gonna sell it, I'm going to give you something you have *to sell!" Joe never backed down from Jack, and Jack just had to beat the crap from him. Gypsy thought he was invulnerable, and he found out that he wasn't.—Bill Behrens*

I kicked him and hit him with a row of chairs. Then I crawled back into the ring.

But just for a second. I was grabbing my ultimate weapon for the night: a baseball bat wrapped in barbed wire.

I took it outside, and smashed it into the side of his head. Then I hit him in the back a few times.

The fans had to know that this wasn't part of the show by now, yelling at the announcers to ring the bell. But then some asshole roared, "Whip that nigger's ass! Whoop that black motherfucker's ass!" and I was fired all the way up again. Every time I heard it, I swung harder. My bat kept smashing into his head, sounding like I was hitting a concrete wall. I hit him with the bat. I hit him with pieces of wood. I stomped him into the ground.

Behind me, that loudmouth was still yelling, "Whip that nigger's ass!" If I could have gotten close to him, he'd have gotten as bad as I was giving Joe.

I was at the edge of the steps, near the curtain. There were about six of us there, glancing at each other like, "Do you want to stop this?" We thought that Joe would be mad! Joe had always told me that he was never going to quit wrestling; he was going to die in the ring. Somebody would stop it, but I wasn't going to be the one if that was what he wanted.—Hammerjack

The promoter finally arrived, telling the crowd that the match had been stopped for unnecessary roughness.

Shit, again, what did they expect? If I'd let him kick my ass, I'd have looked like an idiot. Fans would have seen right through it, and I'd have gotten laughed out of the arena. The scumbags in the crowd would have been cheering him on for beating up a black man, and I'd look like I'd taken part in some dog-and-pony white supremacy show! I'd have been everything but a fucking minstrel! I couldn't have that shit.

Somebody came up and told me the cops were coming. I ran to my buddy's car and jumped in the trunk. He drove me up to the highway, and I got into another car and drove back to the hotel.

Joe walked up to Jack like nothing happened, and said, "Thanks for the match." Jack stood up and said, "Are you crazy, you old motherfucker? Get the fuck out of my face!"
Joe wrestled again a few days later.—Hammerjack

Yeah, he recovered. Even kept wrestling for a few more years before he died in 2016. Once he came back from the shitkicking I'd given him, he went on *YouTube* and cut some promos, saying he was going to kill me.

I couldn't stop laughing. No way was I going back there. People would have been ready for me to destroy him again, and I would have, but I'd probably have gotten shot, or maybe even lynched. After a beating like that, wrestling logic would say he'd have to get the revenge victory over me, and I would allow that to happen only when a man landed on the sun.

People say I should give the guy credit for taking my punishment and wrestling for another few years. No, not really. Guys like Gypsy Joe, who keep going long after they should, shame the business that made them great. That guy was the very reason why the business looks bad sometimes. No one's going to buy it if some senior citizen beats up a young, strong guy, and the guy who just sold for the old guy loses his credibility. I've seen way too many guys who only get by because of their name and their past in the ring way beyond when they should be out, and it's sad when you see young guys bouncing around the ring for them. These youngsters are convinced that it's such an honor to get beaten up by someone they grew up idolizing, but they're not thinking about their own future. If he can't beat a guy older than his dad, how's anyone supposed to take it seriously when he fights someone his own age and size? Things like that can and will do serious damage to a career before it has a chance to start.

40

CZW

All of us who went there, in person or by screen, and I'm talking millions of people, will always have a special spot for that run-down, poorly electrified building right near the corner of South Swanson Street. To a city newcomer, it might not look too out of place in a less-than-luxurious part of town, its view almost hidden by one of Philadelphia's largest overpasses. It's been called Viking Hall, the Asylum Arena, and today, plain old 2300 Arena, and without a closer look, one might mistake it for a warehouse or old storage building that people couldn't be bothered to keep all the way up.

That building was the birthplace of the promotion that changed wrestling forever and the careers of so many who made it do so. Any wrestling fan worth much from the past thirty years will recognize it fast. For so many, it will always be the ECW Arena.

I'll tell you time and again that my appearances these days are about money first, and when I stepped back in my old stomping (and slamming and diving) grounds for Combat Zone Wrestling in the last weeks of 2003, I might have even believed it. Today, though, I look back and think there might have been some sentiment involved. It's like when I wrestled for XPW: kicking some Grimes ass was my main motivation, but the times I got to come "home" to the old place felt special as well.

I remember my first impression of CZW, and it was a great preview of why that federation, like XPW, was a watered-down version of my former workplace. I saw one of the main guys climb up on a building and load another guy on his shoulders.

Then he jumped off—right into a pickup full of light bulbs. I was like, what the fuck? Who was that going to impress? I'm sure people had used words like that about me in the past.

Appearance-wise, the *Cage of Death* event wasn't a big deal (well, not for a guy who'd been going hardcore for years). CZW's personal version of *Wrestlemania*, this one had thousands of thumbtacks, a huge cage, weaponry, all sorts of shit that ECW had done first and so much more effectively. *Suspension*, the fifth annual edition of the event, would be the first non-singles match in *Death* history, and they needed a big name along with the change.

Being the "Mystery Partner" in a match is an extra burden for a performer; the company took a chance that only cluing fans in on your appearance would be enough to sell tickets, and now you damned well better come through for everybody.

In the midst of a ten-man cage match (my buddy Messiah was on the other side), like the legendary Wargames matches from 1980s NWA action, I strolled out, my music and the crowd's noise competing for volume. I sauntered down the scaffold several feet above the ring and pounded the hell out of an opponent with fists and garbage cans.

Then I reached into my pocket and yanked out a huge knife. Was I going to make the Mass Transit incident look like a papercut on these guys? Maybe get some practice for the infamous Florida incident that we'll be talking about soon?

No way. I just jumped down into the ring. Then I turned against my teammates, eventually finishing one off with a tabled jump off the top of the cage.

Ironically, despite my treasonous efforts against my own squad, we actually won when some reluctant "colleagues" of mine eliminated the other side! Talk about a win-win!

That was probably my most visible CZW appearance, but I still showed up for them here and there and still got New Jack–crazy on their asses.

> *New Jack and I were in a three-way match with a new guy who was not very good. Jack got hold of a Wolverine-style, three-blade thing that looked like it would kill a man with one swipe, and he started walking toward that guy. I got in front of the guy and pushed New Jack with my shoulder, and took the swipe myself, because I knew New Jack would have killed that guy.—longtime hardcore star Madman Pondo*

Over the years, I've seen so many of these federations that call themselves "extreme" flare up and fall by the wayside, and I'm not sure why this sort of bullshit still happens. I wish to hell it didn't, because it's not doing a damn thing other than ending careers before they can start.

Making it to the big leagues might not necessarily be these guys' motivation, not for all of them, but if it is, doing that kind of thing does nothing but hurt their chances. Promoters, those that actually carry an ounce of power, prestige, and credibility in the business, don't want their names on some guy who can't do anything but get hardcore. Getting slammed on lightbulbs and thumbtacks, having someone set you on fire, and, as I found out the hard way, smashing through a stack of tables isn't going to raise your worth in a promoter's eyes. These guys want ability, not recklessness and a high pain tolerance.

Look, when ECW kicked things to the stratosphere, we were doing things nobody had ever seen before. No one had dived off shit like I was doing. Once they saw us doing it—and succeeding at it—they started trying to copy us, but it never worked. It's OK to have blood and guts sprinkled up and down your card, but not the same thing every match. Anything can get repetitive, and wrestling fans aren't known for being too gifted in patience or attention spans.

Yes, ECW had more than its share of blood and guts, but it had other things as well. It was a three-ring circus, not a one-ring show. Between hardcore matches, you had guys who could truly wrestle. Sometimes that ended up taking just as much of the match, if not more, than the stuff that gave ECW its name. These guys could get nuts at times, but they could also do more.

It's these guys that make it to the next level, not the ones who jump off a cage onto a bare pavement floor and think they're entertaining—like too many guys I'd met in XPW, and then in CZW.

41

TNA

Jack has always had a unique, cool vibe around him, even when I first met him back in Memphis. In the early days of TNA, every week, or every few weeks, we were doing surprises, and he fit that bill as good as anyone. I was all about the surprises, the creative team talking about him and Shark Boy, and for me, that was gold. When you're around Jack, what you see on camera is an extension of his personality, with the ECW vibe and the craziness vibe. But equally as an extension, he's a very entertaining guy to be around in the dressing room. He's outgoing, talkative, opinionated, everything that makes a unique talent. I knew that if he got into it, it would be gold. Shark Boy was so good at his role, I knew it would be entertaining. It was out of both of their wheelhouse, and they did it great. —Jeff Jarrett

Heading into TNA, I was looking to further my career in the same manner I'd kicked it off over a decade before in Georgia—the lure of the small screen.

It's pretty easy for fans to keep track of their favorites all over the Internet, with websites putting up match results as soon as the bell rings and potential cards everywhere, but promoters don't have time to sit around in front of a monitor typing and clicking. If you're going to get in good and keep your name good with the people that might give you a paycheck, you've got to be easy to see. That's tougher and tougher in a world where people don't hardly watch television anymore. TNA was my answer.

Jack wanted to stay on TV, and TNA gave him an opportunity to get on TV. I was trying to get him to stop bumping, which was an ongoing battle he and I had when he was doing indie shows. He still thought he had to be the guy that

41. TNA

dove off the balconies, and he had already been badly hurt. When he worked with me, he was more of a talker and a walk-around fighter, rather than a bumper.—Bill Behrens

My agent called one day, and told me that Jeff Jarrett wanted me to come work at TNA. I was more than a little surprised. Just like the issues with Brian Christopher, I'd never really gotten on well with Jeff—always thought he was riding his dad's coattails all the way to wrestling success. But TV's TV, and when people see you there, they think you might be a good investment; even if I didn't stick, which I figured from the start, I might get some others to want to put New Jack on their banners.

Or maybe they'd want to *not* hire me. After a while, it looked like that was what the higher-ups at TNA had had in mind all along.

It's a self-fulfilling prophecy. If you do it, and it becomes your thing, unfortunately, you start to believe that it's what you have to do. Jack was convinced that he had to keep jumping off balconies and getting hurt. When I brought Jack into TNA, I told them to just play his music. He was in a battle royal, and he was going to go in, punch a bunch of people, and get out. I told Jarrett, "People are going to react as soon as they hear the music." They did. Jeff was a little skeptical because of Jack's rep, and I said I'd babysit him. After the battle royal, it was clear that Jack was over with the people.—Bill Behrens

Right off the bell, it was obvious that someone was trying to water down the ECW crew. I was working with Sabu, Sandman, even Kronus's old partner Perry Saturn, but we had to do it TNA's way—and that meant the opposite of extreme. Weapons, blood, all the crazy-ass shit that fans had loved us for back under Heyman's roof was all but sacrilegious in Jarrett's world, and fans weren't going to get revved up and cheer for the PG-rated version of our work when they'd already seen the adult edition.

It was me, New Jack, Perry Saturn, and some other people. They brought in a bunch of ECW guys to fight the TNA faction. We're going to do an angle with Jeff Jarrett, and the first thing that Jeff Jarrett wants to go is beat all of us up. Jeff's like, "OK, I'm going to grab a chair and hit all of you guys." New Jack and I just looked at each other and started

laughing. We all just went, "No, we're not doing that." If
you're bringing us in as a faction to fight another faction
for your company, and the first thing they have you do is
have one guy beat four of us up, it makes no sense. We're
not going to have one guy beat us all up and then have us
go against your faction later.—Sandman

That wasn't the only reason it was tough for the old crew to come to work with the same passion we'd had years before either. Backstage, as if this needs repeating, Paul E. didn't give a shit what we did as long as we A) didn't get arrested, and B) made it to the next show straight enough to perform. In TNA, people were tiptoeing around backstage on eggshells, scared that they might piss off Jarrett or someone else near the top and get shown the door. WCW was gone, ECW was gone, and the WWE could afford to say to pretty much every wrestler in the business, "We'll pay you as little as we want to, because you don't have another option."

It was all a bunch of bullshit. Just political games. You had to play the politically correct game to play your job. No one who'd been in ECW was going to last long under that kind of a microscope.

I didn't really talk to anyone—just went in there, sat in my locker room spot, went out to the ring, did my thing, and came right back home. By this point, I wasn't there to be making friends with my co-workers or hanging out with them afterward; I'd gotten all that out of my system at ECW. I knew enough about the ins and outs of a wrestling locker room that I didn't have to put on any facades to get along there.

I was driving up from Atlanta to Memphis every week, just like I had been when I was back at Smoky Mountain. And yes, I was still doing a few drugs here and there.

TNA had some drug problems, but nowhere near as much
as in ECW. Jack used to do a ha-ha thing where he'd put
powdered sugar under his nose and see how people would
react. It looked like he'd been snorting all day.—Bill Behrens

But I kept going, hoping to stay there long enough to get noticed by someone better. Then things went even farther south. Rather, certain people running the show tried to push them that way.

They might have been scared that an outsider like me would just out-work everyone, or maybe just wanted to see if they could be the guys that would put a leash around New Jack's neck and corral him.

They knew, as well as anyone else, that I wasn't there to do comedy. If they didn't know that I wasn't there to clown around before the mess with Gypsy Joe, I don't know how they couldn't figure it out by then. But that's what they gave me.

Just a few months before, the WWE had pulled the whole "crazy tag team partners who somehow end up best friends" angle with Booker T and Goldust. Now TNA was mooching it with me.

I didn't know Shark Boy, hadn't really heard of him. But he was a cool kid. If we had to do silly shit, he was cool about it.

> *I had never worked the violent, street-brawl stuff New Jack worked, so when they told me what they were doing, I was scared to death. Any time you work with someone in wrestling, you end up fighting them, so I was scared. I figured he would hate it. Neither one went into it expecting very much. He came over to me, and said, "Look what the fuck they got us doing!" I said, "Yeah, it's ridiculous." I'd rather get on his good side right away.—Shark Boy*

New Jack was playing Candyland on national TV. Goddamn, it feels insane to even write that right now. But I did it. We did it. I almost had to whale him over whose gingerbread man was on the right color. He goaded me into Chutes and Ladders. He pulled me onto a Twister mat.

I wasn't having it. I let this guy know I didn't need him, didn't want him, had no use for him—and, since he didn't talk, I had to fill up the entire argument myself. But as we kept going, it looked like the finned man might just find a way to New Jack's heart after all.

> *After we did the Candyland skit, we were both laughing at the end of it. By the time we got into it, we were laughing about it. It connected us in a weird way that we never expected. You couldn't get two more diametrically opposed characters: you had the guy from the streets, and I was more like a cartoon character.—Shark Boy*

And after a while, yeah, I admit I did get to enjoy it. I explained to him that he needed to get out there and watch my back for a match, but he insisted (again, without talking!) that I join him in a kiddie pool. Not really a black man's typical pastime, but I did, and then he backed me up. If he could mess around once in a while, I could too.

Shark Boy was liking it, I was liking it, and the fans were liking it too. He got me to wear one of his masks during a tag match, and I put it on backward and looked out the earholes. The fans were laughing. If the bosses were trying to embarrass me out of the company, and the business, it was backfiring on them.

They couldn't have that. One night, I carried a sickle that the Grim Reaper himself would have been proud of out to the ring and worked my opponent over with it.

"That's unbelievable," Jarrett told me, and didn't mean it as a compliment. "People aren't going to believe you're stabbing him with a sickle, so don't bring it to the ring anymore."

I didn't. The next week, I carried something else. I don't even remember what it was, but it didn't help his impression of me.

The next week, I headed into Nashville for TV. As soon as I got there, word came to the dressing room that Jarrett wanted to talk to me. With the Bruise Brothers there to save his ass if things got going, he suddenly grew the guts to say something to my face.

"You just don't want to cooperate," he informed me. "Every time I tell you to do something, you do the opposite. You don't let anybody tell you what to do. We're going to have to let you go."

TNA was such a revolving door, not just with New Jack, but with all sorts of talent. I never made a conscious decision that it wasn't working out with New Jack, and I don't think anyone in creative made such a decision. It wasn't any one incident. You could go down the roster of guys that were in and out; that talent door was such a revolving door in those early years.—Jeff Jarrett

I don't know what he expected. Did he think I was going to drop to my knees and beg to stay, pleading with him to let me work, promising to change who I was ... for him?

Nothing happened. He wrote me my check, and I walked out. Like always, I didn't give a fuck.

My only regret for the whole situation was that I didn't get to say goodbye to Shark Boy. I just left too fast. But I've seen him a few times over the years, and we're cool now. He's a cool kid.

I showed up one week, and suddenly I had a new partner. I was disappointed; New Jack and I could have gone on much longer. We didn't get to finish that story.—Shark Boy

41. TNA

I'll give TNA the credit where it's due, however. Almost a decade after ECW went under, and five long years after I got rooked out of appearing at the WWE's *One Night Only* show, I got a call from Tommy Dreamer, letting me know that TNA was bringing back some extremists for its own reunion.

As many issues as I'd had with Jarrett before, Dixie Carter, who was running the show at the time, was awesome.

"Oh, New Jack, you look so great!" she'd gushed when we'd met. "You're in shape." I had a feeling that it was her who'd persuaded Dreamer to get in touch with me; he was OK, but I'm fairly sure he wouldn't have contacted me on his own.

I got some new ring gear and headed into TNA's Impact Zone in Orlando, a slightly cleaner version of the Philly stomping grounds, for *Hardcore Justice.* As the Dudleys came out on top of Balls and Axl, some familiar music hit, and Mustafa and I charged in, our familiar weaponry and attack plans in full effect.

I hadn't gotten to wrestle, but I didn't mind. As long as I was a part of the show and in front of the cameras, I was fine with it. Run-ins and sneak attacks had been my act for so long that it was what the people expected.

I even took a page from Jarrett's book, blasting a guitar through someone's head. Then everyone got up and hugged. After this long fighting, it was OK to admit that time heals all wounds, even if we had to inflict some shortly beforehand.

In a weird sort of way, just as knocking the hell out of Mustafa had helped me get rid of my issues with him, this sort of beatdown did a lot to fix my issues with the Dudleys. So much time passing has played a big role in this, but things like this help you take some steps toward reconciliation.

Yeah—only in the wrestling world could smashing a guy's head in actually *save* your relationship with him!

42

The Florida Stabbing

Did you think I *wasn't* going to talk about this? Even *brag* about it?

Just a year after everybody was screaming about what a *bully* I was, how *mean* and *cruel* I was for beating the shit out of Gypsy Joe, there came another incident—one that proved again how little of a fuck I'll ever give about how certain Internet loudmouths and much of the general public feel about New Jack.

I got a call from the people in Florida's Thunder Wrestler Federation in October 2004, asking if I'd drive south from my then–Georgia home to do a show for them.

Specifically, a hardcore weapons match. I said that would be fine.

They assured me that I wouldn't have any problems, and I agreed. At least, that's what I told them on the phone. Inside, I was already cracking up. What, did they think I was going to get beat up, with or without my consent?

I showed up at the hotel in Jacksonville, hanging out in the audience chairs with my old ECW brother Hack Meyers and some other people I don't remember. Then some guy who I'd never seen before came strolling up to us like he'd been in the business forever.

"You want to go over the match, right?" he coolly queried. OK, so this is the guy I'm working with, I now guess. With Gypsy Joe, I'd been wrestling a guy who'd been in the business about three *generations* too long; now I was up against a guy who'd had a handful of matches and thought he knew something. Still, I was cool about it.

"Kayfabe, bro!" I responded. "Just give me a minute." He smacked the table we were sitting at.

"What the fuck ever...." he came back.

Oh no. No, you don't talk like that to people who've been in the business a fuck of a lot longer than you. You also don't talk to me like that, period. Either this guy seriously overestimated his own tenacity or didn't know who he was chatting with.

168

42. The Florida Stabbing

Shit was about to get even more real. And very, very painful.

I found a buddy with some drugs to buy. I bought an 8-ball. I snorted it. Then I thought about all the ways I could hurt this guy. Even take him out forever.

Just like with Joe, the chairs at that hotel were more empty than full. And just like with Joe, it didn't take long for things to get royally fucked up.

He hit me a few times in the eyes and mouth, and I grabbed him and backed him against the ropes. We stood there, and stood there, and stood there. I'm sure the crowd figured that someone had screwed up. They were right, but not the in the way they thought.

I reached into a pocket on my pants, and pulled out a Wolverine-type claw, with one of the blades having broken off.

I stuck him in the sides, in the shoulders. It didn't take him long to figure out what was going on, but he couldn't get away.

He went down as I slashed him some more. Then he got to his knees, and my knee smashed into his face, knocking him out of the ring.

I stabbed him a few more times, and my blade started getting in a bit deeper. I could see some people standing up and backing away; looks like this was even more real than they'd expected. I stood on his head for a few minutes, getting bored with it all.

The promoter and a couple of other guys came out to try to pull me off. Yeah, right. I'd just stabbed the hell out of a guy—did they think I was just going to let everything go, hand out the high-fives, and walk away? Not happening.

Anyway, as crazy as this got, it never went as far out of control as people made it out to be. First off, I stabbed the guy nine times—might not sound like a huge difference, but people tried to make it like fifteen or twenty. I stabbed him as many times as I wanted, and I counted it. People made it sound like I was some bloodthirsty madman or something, trying to kill a guy in public over a wrestling match that *maybe* a few hundred people would see: not expecting, of course, that someone would be standing there with a cell phone, broadcasting it all over the Internet!

Still high as hell, I wandered back to the dressing room, and just *happened* to run into a couple of cops. With the cocaine holding too tight for me to hardly be able to comprehend what was going on, I felt my hands getting cuffed behind my back, getting hauled off to the jail, getting my picture taken, and being escorted straight to a cell.

Then I realized that with all my knife action, I'd managed to cut the hell out of my arm, deep enough that I had to go straight to the hospital.

There I was, lying in a bed in an ER, stitches in my arm, and a worker came up to my bed.

"Hey, man," he whispered, like he had a huge bit of confidentiality to share. "That guy you stabbed is like two doors down!"

I laughed and shook my head. Then I heard someone yelling up the hall.

"New Jack," called a familiar voice, "you all right?"

"I'm just fine," I sarcastically responded, still fighting off a laugh. "You all right?"

"Yeah," he said. "A couple of holes, but I'm all right." In a weird sort of way, he sounded disappointed.

Back I went to jail, and I sat there for weeks. Then one of my more computer-literate fans got the Internet behind me for one of the first, and still strongest times of my career. She set up a website to raise enough dough to get me out of the clink.

"Free New Jack!" she wrote on the site. "If you're his so-called friends, let's see you step up now!" They responded, chipping in over $4,000 to "save" a guy they'd only known through a television ring persona.

Then some guy from the district attorney's office showed up. "We'll offer you twelve years," he said, downplaying it, like he was doing me a favor, trying to lull me into a sense of comfort like these guys usually do. I guess he figured I'd never debated with a lawyer before.

"I'm not doing that," I responded. I wasn't sure how this was going to turn out, but it had been a wrestling match. My opponent and the guys behind the scenes had been all but begging for a hardcore match, and they might have gotten more than they'd expected, but hell, I was New Jack after all. Just another example of how you can do shit in a ring that you never could in real life.

But I'd get some help from about the most unexpected—but not really, all things considered—span of allies. As I sat in my cell one day, a guard showed up to tell me I had a visitor.

I sat down at the visiting spot, and could hardly believe who was across from me.

My old opponent.

Was he going to try to get revenge right then and there? Was he going to rub in my face that I was going to jail for even longer than I'd been offered, and that he was behind it all? Not quite.

"Jack," he inquired, "how can we make this go away?"

I could hardly believe it. But I couldn't show that. If I looked too eager,

I might say something I'd regret, or give myself away. I had to make it look like he actually *was* doing me a favor.

"What if I drop the charges, and you train me?" he asked. "We'll take this on the road: 'He's gunning for New Jack!'"

I thought about it. Pretended I was thinking about it. Really, I was just considering how I could spin this all the way to my advantage.

"OK, OK," I acted like I was agreeing. "But you got to drop the charges first." I couldn't believe how fast he agreed.

Right after that, he was out at the courthouse. Not long after that, I was on my way to court myself. As I stepped out of an elevator, the district attorney was standing right there with a little piece of paper.

"Your charges have been dropped," he said, as grudgingly as anyone had ever said a word. "You're free to go."

I signed the paper, handed him a mile-wide smile as full of spite as I could stretch it, and sauntered out of the building.

Oh, about all that money raised on the Internet for my bail? I never had to pay the bail, so I kept it. It was amazing how friendly the fans were about it, even after their money stayed with me.

People sent me their addresses, their personal phone numbers. "I'm glad I could help you out!" they'd write. "If you can't get in touch with me, here's my wife's number. If you need anything, call me." I don't know what it was about New Jack that made people want to go so far to help him out, but I didn't really care. It was some of the easiest money I'd ever made.

It's pretty amazing how far out of their way people will go for you if they see you on TV, or your name on a website or something. I've been seeing that my whole career, probably most of all (before Florida) being my time in ECW, where ring rats paid for my rooms and cars and brought me booze and drugs and everything else. These people might have been better off than I was or might have been barely making it, but they did so much for a guy whose real name many of them would never know.

I guess it just makes them feel important. They feel good about themselves. They could give their money to charity, they could volunteer for a cause or some sort of event, or they could give money to a wrestler. Amazing how many went for the last option.

Always a man of my word, I went home from jail, immediately got in touch with my former opponent, and started training him. Mere months later, he was selling out arenas, headlining *Wrestlemania*, and becoming the biggest star the wrestling world has ever seen! You heard his name a million times in 2019!

Oh, wait, no you haven't. I never trained him at all. I don't know if he ever wrestled again. I went home, but I sure as shit didn't call him.

I packed up all my clothes, put my big stuff in storage, and moved. Shortly thereafter, I was living up in Cincinnati. I've still never been back to Florida (or wrestled in Tennessee), but I don't give a fuck. Those places were never a fan base for me, and, after more than a quarter-century in the business, I'm not exactly looking to break back out.

Still, I'm not a complete liar. I did call the guy—a few years later.

"Cases like this, they put them on *Judge Mathis*," I told him, talking about one of my favorite shows. "They'll pay you up to five thousand! Why don't we go on *Judge Mathis*? I'll act like the biggest dick in the world, you'll get paid, and we'll split the money!" Talk about a package deal.

"I can't do it," he admitted. "I'm too embarrassed." To this day, I've never heard from him again.

As you've probably figured out by now, regret and remorse really aren't in New Jack's vocabulary. Like Gypsy Joe before him, this guy knew what he was getting into, and he got it. Then he got paid back for it and gave me interest. Interest in a career that continues today and a place in infamy that I'll never let go of.

Not that I'd ever fucking want to.

43

My Fighting Career

Me and Jack are boys, and to me, if you're boys, you can't be friends with someone that you're friends with all *the time. You have a tight situation at some point. He came back to the locker room, and I said something to him; we were both high. He had a beer bottle. He threw it at me, I got my arm up, and the beer bottle shattered on my wrist. We tussled for a little bit, and the whole room broke us up. It was all over something stupid. It only lasted fifteen seconds.—Sandman*

Looking back over all the violence I have described in this book, both in and out of the ring, I feel like I really need to make a point here about my so-called thuggish reputation. You go all over the Internet and you hear this shit about me being crazy, me being violent, me hurting so many sweet, pure, innocent people just because it's fun. Let me tell you something about that garbage—people get awfully gusty when they have a screen to hide behind and don't have to amp up the balls to say something to your face.

It's bullshit. I don't feel like I'm any more violent than most people, who don't have to worry about winding up on the electronic tabloids every time they give somebody a dirty look.

You've read about quite a few brawls that I've been through in these pages, and there are plenty more that you never will. But every time I have gotten into a fight with anybody—*every time*—it was because they did something to make me do it. From defending myself against people who thought it was fun to pick on the new guy in town when I was a kid to squaring off in and out of the ring and locker room during my wrestling career, I've been drawn in to trouble. We can all look back and think of times where we've been in the wrong place around the wrong people at the wrong time, and maybe that's happened to me more than most people, but, again, it's happened to us all.

It's not that hard. I'm not a tough person to work with, in the business sense or the personal sense. For every person who's gotten hurt in a match with me, there's hundreds who will tell you that I took care of them, usually better than I did of myself.

I feel like I've earned the right to say to other, much less experienced wrestlers, just don't disrespect me. Don't tell me what we're going to do because I don't want to hear it. If I'm the veteran, and you're new to the scene, don't come up to me with your stupid-ass ideas.

Other guys who have been through the ring wars might have a more eloquent way of saying that, but it's a common mindset in wrestling. Sometimes guys step right into a new federation, right out of school, and think that they're the new thing, that they know everything and that they can save the company, but that's not how you get started in a new place. You listen, you learn, you shut up. Eventually, you get the right to speak up and offer ideas, but it's going to take a while. It's takes even longer to get to where you can lead. Guys (and gals!) who have been busting their asses in a tough business don't want to take lessons from newcomers.

Paul E. always pointed out just how politically incorrect I was (talk about the pot and the fucking kettle!). I told him he was right. Absolutely right. I just don't tolerate bullshit and I never have. Whatever I did to someone, they caused me to do it.

44.

Wildside

You've seen Bill Behrens's name quite a bit throughout this book. Here are a few reasons why.

Back when the Gangstas were starting out in Smoky Mountain, a guy came up to us and asked if he could snap a picture of us. Sure, why would we say no to that?

So we stepped into character, and so did he. Then we got to chatting with this Bill fellow.

He'd been around the business a bit longer than us. He was in good with many of the people that could sign our paychecks, in SMW and elsewhere. As you've probably guessed by now, negotiating isn't really a strong suit of mine, and in a business such as wrestling, where there are so many "employees" and so few positions available, anyone's replaceable. You need a guy to talk to other guys for you, and then you go in the ring and do the heavy shit.

So I eventually asked Bill to be my negotiator, and now I'm part of one of the biggest client lists in wrestling. But even today, people in wrestling know his word's good, so they call and try to get his clients. It's up to us to keep making his word mean something, and I feel like I've done OK with that.

Along with all the deals that Bill's made for me, one of them has been a little more personal. That was his NWA Wildside promotion that I started cameoing for in the last years of ECW.

Whenever I had some time off, I'd head to Cornelia, just outside of Atlanta, and do my thing for his company, next to guys like Matt Hardy, A.J. Styles, and some others who were moving in and out of wrestling's major leagues. After ECW went down, that, of course, became even more important. I'd go there whenever I could, getting on some small TV shows here and there. I'd wrestle, cut promos and interviews, do what I could. Wildside was a masterpiece of doing a ton with very little (money, exposure, prestige, etc.), so I did what I could for it. Even when I was in the

175

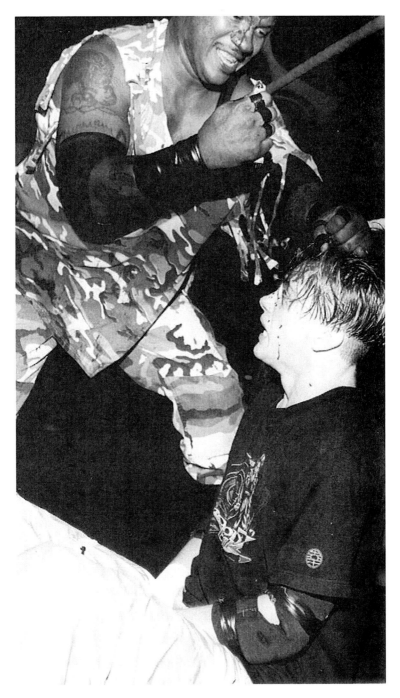

middle of everything else in wrestling, I wanted to stay in the ring and on the screen.

Hell, Bill even let me move into his house for a few weeks right around the time I left XPW, so, yeah, I'd say this guy deserved some serious loyalty!

Bill wasn't going to ask me to go anywhere near the extremes that I'd gone just about everywhere else, but sometimes I let myself get a little crazy there too.

Live on TV, I was supposed to get into a makeshift hit and run, a guy in a truck trying to run me down and me charging after him. Wildside didn't have the time or money to do take after take, but I'd never needed that for my promos, so why for a vignette? In hindsight, I probably let my pride blow my ego out a bit there.

When the call for action came, I stormed into the parking lot, ready to take on the trucker. Just one problem—the truck was right there idling. It was supposed to start off coming right at me; if it did it now, it would look contrived as hell. We couldn't cut away. We couldn't call cut.

I ran up behind the truck, just as it finally started to move. I grabbed hold of the trailer hitch, about to climb up and go to work. Or maybe flip it over, slash its tires, kick out its exhaust, whatever the hell.

Then, though, it picked up. Like a true extreme icon, I didn't let go. As it accelerated, I was back there, getting dragged behind a truck because I was too into it (or too stupid!) to drop my grip.

About twenty feet later, I finally realized what I was doing, and released the truck. Then I fell straight into a mud puddle about the size of Lake Ontario.

I went up and said, "Jack, you OK?" He said, "My underwear's all gooey. Do you have any I can borrow?"—Bill Behrens

---

Of course, my time in Wildside wasn't without my usual issues. One day, I cut a promo that—I don't mind bragging to you—was one of my finest ever. I stepped in front of a camera and let my pseudo-audience know exactly what I was going to do to my opponent and why they needed to tune in or walk in and see it. I was gonna give this guy everything he could handle and then so much more. I finished up and stepped away, just hoping I could back up everything I'd blabbed about.

Opposite: **Getting Jimmy Rave a little color at a NWA Wildside match.**

Then my opponent stepped in. He couldn't have fucked it up worse if he'd stood there and shouted, "This match is going to suck! Stay home or change your channel!" It was horrible, one of the worst I'd ever seen or heard, one I was embarrassed to be alongside on the show. It completely ruined what I'd just put so much heat and heart into.

So fucking angry, I became my own first victim. Ready to tune this guy all the way up, I inadvertently sliced my hand open. The only thing that kept me from taking it to him right then and there was someone else's fear that I might bleed out in the process!

> *Jack's in the back bleeding, and our nurse is holding onto his hand, trying to bandage him up. Jack's yelling at me, trying to gesticulate with his hands simultaneously, throwing this poor woman around.—Bill Behrens*

I wasn't done. My hand finally as cleaned as the nurse could make it, I went outside and found the guy.

Then I took him down, landed a few bombs, and went to yank his eyeball right out of its socket. You don't fuck with New Jack's promos.

> *Another guy and I got on either side of Jack and pulled him off. Jack said, "Thank God you did that. I was blown up!"—Bill Behrens*

It was more funny than anything. I'd just wrestled at the show, and now I had to go and get involved in something like that.

I don't remember if I knew about it in advance, but I got wild one last time on April 30, 2005, as the Wildside promotion said goodbye with its *Last Rites* show. After being away for a while, I stepped into a WarGames match as a surprise partner to become a part of the federation's last winning team. Then I said goodbye the same way I always had: by grabbing a microphone and ad-libbing my ass off.

Everyone was crying and hugging, and Bill got lifted into the air, but I have to be honest: I didn't even really feel that much during the event, or during the match itself. I just did what I wanted and left, knowing I'd just have to find another place to get on TV. Other people might have seen that night as some kind of deeply moving moment, but I wasn't thinking that way.

44. Wildside

That's not to say I'm glad I feel that way. Sometimes I wish that things like that could affect me a little more. It might be the physical or emotional pain that I'll always feel from wrestling, or just moving around so much for personal and professional reasons that I don't really become attached to people or places. Maybe that will change someday, and I don't think I'd mind it.

45

The Benoit Murders

I didn't really react at first. How the fuck can you? How can anyone?

When you find out that a lady you'd known for over a decade, who had been one of your closest co-workers for years, who you'd seen just a few months before, just got murdered by her asshole of a husband, you're supposed to...?

Yeah, I'm pretty sure no one's ever asked themselves that question and come up with a legit answer. I didn't. That's why it didn't really click with me when I found out that that dirtbag Chris Benoit had murdered his wife and son in June 2007.

I didn't give a fuck about that guy. He'd been kind of jerk in ECW, always ignoring everybody, walking around like he just knew he was better than everybody else. His wife, Nancy, was the greatest, hanging out with us, just great to be around, someone everyone loved.

When I first heard, I was thinking more about the douchebag killing his son. How the fuck do you do that? That kid was seven years old. I don't care what kind of problems Benoit was having, what kind of kid Daniel was, whatever. The child shouldn't have died. His wife shouldn't have died. If Benoit was pissed off enough to kill, he should have just taken his own life—which he did, after murdering them—and let them live. Believe me: they'd have been *much* better off without him.

But, again, when I first heard, the first thing in my mind was how the *fuck* someone does that to his own son! I didn't put two and two together at first. Then it hit me: He was married to Nancy.

Nancy, who'd been married to my friend Kevin Sullivan, a guy who'd tried to get me into WCW. Nancy, who was so great to everyone in the ECW locker room. Nancy, just another one of the guys, a hell of a lot more so than her husband. In the *business* longer than her husband. Because of this cowardly piece of shit, she was gone.

And he was too, fortunately. But from the way people talked, you'd think he was the only one who had died, or that he was just an innocent victim in it all. People talked about what a great wrestler he was, what an inspiration he'd been to many young wrestlers, how hard he'd worked, and all that garbage.

Bullshit. I called bullshit when I first heard that mess, and I still do. He was a great wrestler? Fuck wrestling! Lots of guys are great wrestlers, and take care of their wives and kids. This guy filled his son up with Xanax and strangled him to death? You want to just brush all of that shit aside and talk about how he could *wrestle*? Dude killed his whole family, and people want to talk about a headlock?

It was disgusting the way so many people basically shit on Nancy. So many people just referred to her as "his wife," "the wife," "the child's mother," whatever. Hardly anybody even said her name.

Nancy was the best. She had Kevin Sullivan, one of the greatest minds in the business, and she was just as good. She was smart as shit about how angles would work. I didn't even know she was teaching me when she was teaching me. We did a blind angle where Tommy Dreamer hit me with the cane. I wanted to do a thing where I would run through the audience and bleed and bleed. Nancy said no, we weren't doing it like that. She said, "When Tommy hits you with that fucking cane, you're going to lie there, and I'm going to stand over you in shock. I'm going to look at the ref, look at you, look up, and everybody's going to freak out, because they'll think it's real." When I found out she was dead, I couldn't move for like two hours.—Sandman

---

And people just kept trying to excuse it, trying to find ways to justify this horrible thing that this pseudo-hero did. It was a case of 'roid rage! No, it wasn't. His wife provoked him! No, she didn't.

What we finally heard, and what so many people still believe today, was that his brain was so beaten to mush that he didn't understand what he was doing. That he couldn't "assess the magnitude" of murdering his own son and wife or some such bullshit.

More and more and more bullshit. He had that diving headbutt, but he hardly ever got hit in the head. I got hit in the head a ton of times, Balls Mahoney got his brains beaten in, the Rottens, Public Enemy, everybody.

Benoit's dad came out and called ECW "garbage wrestling," and talked all that shit about Benoit getting hit in the head so many times that he couldn't tell right from wrong.

I saw it all for myself. If Benoit had to get hit with a chair, he *always* had his hands in front of it. He hardly ever got hit in the head by *anything*, let alone a steel chair. Of all the guys I worked with in ECW, he got hit less than almost anyone. He was a chickenshit coward in the ring, and an even bigger one out of it.

'Roid rage? Another load of shit. I've known plenty of people who have done steroids and not turned into murderers. Yes, I've done them myself for a while, and you know what it did to me? Acne on my back! It didn't make me go psycho on my girlfriends or wives, my kids, or anyone else, even in the ring. People blame shit like that on steroids, but it's garbage.

Chris Benoit, along with his buddy Dean Malenko, was always one of those guys who thought he was too good to get in the ring with me. I had made it known that I wasn't going to lie down for them, mainly because I didn't like them. They'd bully the new guys coming in, guys trying to make their name in the business just like Benoit did, and I didn't go for that shit. They knew that I didn't like them, they knew that I wasn't going to go out of my way and sacrifice myself to make them look good, so they didn't want to try it on with New Jack. Just guys who put their own interests above anyone and anything else.

And if I didn't have enough to get upset about by the Benoit killings, less than a month later, I got a phone call that my old teammate John Kronus was gone too. Unlike the Benoit case, though, this one was sad as shit, but not really a surprise. Just in his late thirties with a young son, John had known for a long time that his heart was too big, and that it was going to fail him at some point, so he always lived like he had nothing to lose—doing drugs, doing crazy shit in the ring. He didn't see it as a risk because he always figured he'd go young anyway, and sadly he was right.

When I heard about that, I did something I'd never done before, or have since. I left my Richmond home, hopped on a train, and rode it up to Rhode Island for the funeral.

And when I walked in, my heart broke all over again. Because I was the only one from ECW at his funeral. Not Paul E. or Tod Gordon. Not his old partner Perry Saturn. Not the Dudleys, the Pit Bulls, or anyone else he'd worked with. Just New Jack.

I'm not saying that to brag, because I sure as shit wish it wasn't a true story. Just a fucked-up fact. Of course, being mobbed by a bunch of asshole fans who thought I'd be in a mood to sign some autographs as my friend lay there in a casket didn't exactly help my state of mind either. I had an urge to give some local funeral homes a few reasons to sell some caskets, but I stayed in check and left, and, no, I didn't write my name anywhere that day.

John wasn't the first wrestling buddy I lost, and he wouldn't be the last. Earlier that year, both my ECW colleagues Bam Bam Bigelow and Mike Awesome had left too soon. Years later, my close friend Nelson Frazier (Mabel, Viscera) was gone. But I've never visited a wrestler's funeral since John's, and I don't intend to.

And if any of my brothers or sisters skip mine, I'll be looking down, deciding who needs one more 187 for their own backstabbing nature.

46

Retirement

I thought I was done. I'd been thinking I was done for a while. I was ready to be done.

The thought of quitting the ring had been on my mind for years. It had been a while since I'd been on anywhere near a full-time schedule, but the times I was in the ring, I was always the New Jack from ECW people remembered and who I thought they really wanted—risk-taking and bone-breaking.

> *Jack's real talent wasn't that he could dive through shit and was fearless, or that he was scary and dangerous in the ring. It's that he had the type of personality that you can't teach. If you've got it, all you can do is fuck up and not use it as much as you should. Jack had a tendency to think that, rather than letting his personality be his moneymaker, that he had to go into the ring and have a weapons match, everything overly hardcore or the crowd wasn't going to be happy.—Bill Behrens*

The end comes for everyone, but that's tough to accept. I don't think I knew just how tough until the first few times I tried it.

I had half-assedly announced I was quitting at a one-shot XPW show in California in May of 2008, but that had lasted about as long as it took me to get back to the dressing room. Mustafa and I had teamed up there yet again, but we hadn't been at the top of the card (a guy named Necro Butcher headlined it, which would end up being pretty ironic). When New Jack went out, it was going to be the night's main event, no matter who got shoved down the undercard.

That, and I wasn't going to have my last wrestling memory be from a hellhole like XPW!

46. Retirement

That was a big question mark in my head about his retiring, but I thought it would be fun to kick it with my brother at least one more time. —Mustafa Saed

---

I could try booking some more, like I did in 2009. I was living in Cincinnati, and a buddy of mine had a weight gym that I started using a lot. He had a large spare room with bleachers, chairs, a ring, everything. Just no fans or athletes.

I went to him with an idea. Why not give it a shot from the other side of the business? I'd been in the ring for so long, but I'd been around the guys who called the shots from backstage, the ones who decided who'd wrestle who, and who'd win. These were the guys whose job it was to guess how the fans would react with one run-in, another finish, a face turn here or a heel turn there.

"Just let me do wrestling shows out of here," I asked my friend. He handed me the rights, and I started working shows. I had some guys in the area who had been in the business for a while come and help me. We had some local guys jump at the chance to get a little time in the ring in front of a crowd.

And the crowds came. Our shows were doing pretty well. We were making it happen.

But then I had to leave. After about six shows, I moved to Pittsburgh.

It was nice to have people at a show do what you say. It shows that they have confidence in you. They listen because they want to. They believe. I haven't booked since then, but never say never.

Back to the independents I went, along with some more CZW stuff. Things had been slowing down for me for a while, and I thought I was ready for them to stop. I couldn't get as crazy as I used to, and there were many other guys, in much better shape and with far fewer years of wear and tear, that could do much more. In my younger years, I'd have shown those motherfuckers up, but prime time was passé for New Jack.

I was just tired of being tired and hurt all the time. I was always going to the doctor, sore as shit, hurting everywhere, and taking longer to feel better. Things that had taken a day to heal started taking weeks. Injuries from years ago were coming back to torment me. Time was near, and it was short.

But I was ready in a lot of other ways as well. I've seen so many of my friends from the business end up not just physically broken, but broken in the financial sense as well. Down and out, living on government handouts, their money and their stability all gone because they never thought about later tonight, let alone tomorrow. So many have gone from living too hard to living check to check. Then the checks stop coming, and you're just shit out of luck, or even out of a home if you really got careless.

And if you're in the wrestling business, you're always on the road, always on the go. You're moving around so much, so fast, that you barely have time to see your families, let alone anyone who might help you prepare for life after wrestling. You get so you don't have time to think about it, so you stop trying to, and just worry about your next match.

I tell everyone I meet who wants to go into wrestling to stay in school as long as possible. Education may not have been a cornerstone for me, but I'll never know if it might have been if I hadn't fucked everything up with my criminal activities. You finish college, you get that degree under you, you're only in your early 20s. You'll have plenty to time to make it in the business, assuming you still want to.

I did, but I did what I could to get ready for the future. I used to joke to my friends that the hardest chokehold I ever gave in my career was to my dollar bills. That's why I could afford to kick back before my legs got too battered to kick at all. I'm not rich, never was, but I'm in pretty safe shape.

All of that was in my mind as I crept down the aisle of New Jersey's Metuchen Sportsplex on the evening of April 5, 2013. The Pro Wrestling Syndicate had spent the past two nights putting on one hell of a super card for the fans there, with everyone from Vader to the Iron Sheik and Jushin Liger to my old ECW cronies Tommy Dreamer, Sandman, and Terry Funk there to perform, but New Jack was going to close out the show.

For the last time. It had been promoted as my finale, my swan song, and I was good to say goodbye.

Bootsy Collins's music hit, and I high-stepped out, my ever-present garbage can full of weapons in one hand, and my staple gun in the other.

And across the ring from me? None other than Necro Butcher.

The promoter called me and said, "New Jack's calling it quits, and he wants to have a match with you." I wouldn't say I knew New Jack well, but I'd worked with him a few times. It's personal pride that a man with his reputation, who could have named his opponent from literally hundreds of wrestlers that could have filled my shoes, would choose me.—Necro Butcher

---

46. Retirement

He butchered me for the first few minutes. Then I yanked out a fork and planted it just above one of his eyes. Pretty soon, there was enough blood on his upper body to repaint half the building. Soon we went outside and started throwing each other through the audience. But no one was going to come running out and whining about excessive violence in this match.

Gushing out some plasma myself, I blasted him in the nuts with a chair. Then he dropped me right into two upright chairs. They didn't bend or break, but I thought my spine had. He went atop the ropes, and I gunned him into a chair of my own.

But I ended with the night's stunner moment, pulling out my scientific side, turning a cradle into a backslide and a small package to...

Yeah, right. Armed with a chair wrapped in light tubes, I jumped off the top rope and planted it right in his face for the three-count. It's tradition for a retiree to put over the new guy as his final thanks to the business, but New Jack specializes in telling tradition to fuck itself. I wasn't passing any torches this night, and Butcher had been fine with that.

Just as I never had before, I hadn't gotten ready for my retirement speech.

"Thank you, New Jack!" fans started to chant, louder and louder.

"Shut your motherfucking asses up!" I kindly requested to the crowd. "Fuck you!" Then I turned to Butcher, as bloody as any opponent I'd ever battled, and looked him square in the eye.

"Thank you," I told him. We hugged and he headed out. As he made his way back toward the dressing room, it emptied into the aisle, my old opponents the Rock 'n' Roll Express at the lead. Now chants of "ECW!" blasted through the crowd.

I told them the story of finding New Jack at the movies. I thanked the PWS crew for having me. Then I addressed my co-stars.

"I'll walk away from this shit before it walks away from me!" I vowed. "At fifty fucking years old, it's time for me to go ahead and let this crew have the wisdom, the knowledge, on how to get paid, how to feed your fucking family!" More chants of "Thank you, New Jack!" came up.

Finally, it was time for the end. As I led the way with the opening lyrics, the crowd belted in for one last rendition of the theme song that Bootsy had put together for me. The Express stepped into the ring for one last hug and salute. I don't know if I've ever had a crowd so into me before that night.

187

New Jack

> *When I'd worked with him back in Smoky Mountain, New Jack caught on quick. But not only that—New Jack became my friend. New Jack is like me; once you get this wrestling business in your blood, it's hard to give it up. You get addicted to it. That's just the way it is. For him to mention on that night that Robert and I helped him, that was one of the most flattering things I'd ever heard.—Ricky Morton*

And that was it. I walked out, mingled with the fans and my guys in the locker room for a while, then hopped on a plane and went home.

And I stayed there for two whole years.

I sat around. I slept all day. I shopped. I watched TV, though not much of the squared circle. I'd go out to the bars and shoot pool if that's what I wanted, or I'd stay home for days on end if the mood struck.

That was it. I was happy there. I thought it would last forever, and I wouldn't have minded in the least.

My phone kept ringing, and I ignored it. People were making offers all the time, hoping I'd show up just for an appearance or one special match, and I always responded in the negative, if I answered at all. I figured all that would stop once word got around that I wasn't in the mood to resurrect New Jack.

But it didn't. Years after I was gone, forever after I had been seen anywhere near a ring, people were still calling for Jack. Some of these calls and offers were more credible than others, but the sheer number showed me that people still gave a fuck.

And something strange happened. I realized that, as hard as I'd worked, I was bored. I didn't want to go back on the road, but I might not mind showing up at a show here and there. It would be easy. Quick work. Sign a few autographs, yell into a microphone, maybe get to punch somebody, and get out and home with a paycheck. What was wrong with that?

That, and I was putting on some serious weight. Didn't want that.

> *It's hard to retire. What is that word, anyway? The boots are in your closet, and you're looking at them, and people keep calling you, it's hard to stay away. The spotlight is always on you, and it's hard to turn it off. When it's on you for the last time, you still feel like you can keep going. There's nothing else like it. It's your dreams coming true. My goal is to keep wrestling until I'm seventy-two!—Mustafa Saed*

46. Retirement

Shit, this is wrestling. Do you think I'd get sued for breaching an agreement if I came back after calling it quits? People bitch all the time about wrestlers not having unions, but one good thing is that nobody can take action against you if you decide to put the tights back on.

When a wrestler says he's retiring, it's about as credible as a movie character getting killed, and then coming back in the sequel. It's ceremonial, not real. People are surprised if you *don't* come back to the ring a few times after you say goodbye. I was in grade school the first time Terry Funk had his farewell tour; as I get close to sixty, he's still at it!

Man, fuck tradition. Me coming back wasn't going to tarnish my legacy. Showing up for a show here and a spot there, I wasn't going to embarrass myself. I had been in the business for over twenty years; if people didn't like me, they weren't going to start, and if they did, they weren't going to stop. I think some of my old-school colleagues overestimate the memory span of wrestling fans these days.

It probably took me *far* too long to realize this, but eventually a wrestler has to rely on his legacy to stay anywhere near the public eye. At some point, you've just got to trust the fans to say, "Hey, I used to watch that New Jack guy all the time! I'd *love* to go out and meet him and see what he's been up to!"

Fans don't expect us in the business, especially those in the ECW clan, to come out and smash through tables and off balconies anymore. Not to downplay anything I or anyone else in ECW did, but it's way too easy to find people willing to break every bone in their body for $5 if it *might* (and 99.999 percent of time it won't) get them noticed by a bigger federation.

Fans of yesterday might look at their old heroes hanging on too long and say, "He's not as great as he used to be, so I'm not going to be a fan of his anymore." I don't think today's fans really feel that way. They see us, they cheer for us, and they don't really think about us until they see us again. It's not better or worse than it used to be for fans and wrestlers and their relationships; it's just the way things are. Maybe it'll be different a generation or a few down the road.

I think it will, and that's something I learned when I started coming back. Hanging out with the young guys in the dressing room, I was meeting the guys who'd grown up in those very stands, cheering for me. I wasn't a great role model for upcoming wrestlers, but just seeing the effort that I'd put in for so long was something that had impressed and inspired them, even years after I'd done it.

New Jack

It's weird to be able to do that. To go out there, get into the ring, win or lose, and find out that you can have that effect on someone. You never know what's going to make a difference for people, how you can inspire someone without knowing it or meaning to. I think that, along with the entertainment and the fanfare, most wrestlers have a spot for that on the priority list. I've been lucky enough to meet quite a few people that see New Jack as more than just a character I played.

47

Meeting and Marrying Jennifer

I wasn't sure if I'd given up on marriage or if it had given up on me, but I didn't really care. I'd gotten married young and it hadn't worked. Then I'd gone through the whole thing again.

For over a decade, I'd slept around and all over. I'd been with women I'd never seen before or would again, some whose name I never learned. I just wasn't thinking about relationships, let alone marriage. Why would I? I was getting laid so much that I'd forgotten all about attraction or love. But all that was over now, and had been for quite a while.

I was with Terri Runnels for about a year and a half right around 2010, but I'm done talking about that. If you came here looking for some dirty shit about us, it's not happening. I've talked about that relationship in about a million interviews all over the Internet, so if you want to hear about it, go find a computer.

Maybe I was scared, maybe I was scarred from the past, maybe I was worried about having to move somewhere or go and do something elsewhere and didn't want to settle down, maybe anything. In any case, I didn't think too much about bringing someone else into my life for years after I cut back on wrestling.

In November 2016, I'd just gotten off a plane from a show in Minnesota, then ridden a bus back to near my then-home in Atlantic City. (If this keeps up, it'll be easier to count the places I *haven't* lived. Moving around all the time is a tactic I carried over from childhood!) Walking up the sidewalk, my leg suddenly started cramping like hell.

I went down, and some shots of agony rolled through my back. I was lucky enough to have a lady walk by at the right time.

"Are you all right?" she asked.

Forget pride or toughness or any of that shit. I told her that no I was not, and that something was seriously wrong with my legs and back.

191

I handed her my cell phone, and she called for an ambulance (if she reads this, *thank you!*). Minutes later, I was in the hospital.

A few days later, I was sent to another. I'd be there for weeks.

They found blood clots in my legs, my back, and one in my lung. I think they may have formed from sitting down on a long flight, one of so many such rides that I've taken.

I sat in the bed for day after day, week after week. No one came. No one called. Of all the people I'd met and known during all my time in wrestling, I didn't hear from any of them. It was strange and it was sad, just as I'd felt when I'd been the only one to show up for Kronus' funeral. Only this time, it might have been me in the casket soon; staying in a hospital that long isn't regular. With so many blood clots all over my body, one could form in, or move to, my heart or brain, and that would be it. With the heart trouble I already had, I could feel myself getting close to the final bell.

I was scared. My daughter offered to come, but I didn't want her to drive all the way up from North Carolina. I didn't know what I would say to anyone who did show, but I certainly would have appreciated them making the effort.

After a few days, I put out a message on the Internet to let everyone know what was up. Of course, fans texted and messaged all kinds of things, cheering me on. OK, some of them decided to take the chance to show what jerks they could be with smart-ass, mocking messages, but you're always going to get that. None of them, though, bothered to show up either.

But one message stood out. It was from a lady named Jennifer. She left me her number, telling me to call her when I got out.

Yeah, she could have been crazy, a stalker, someone just posing as a fan, ready to play some kind of sick joke. But I thought it was nice of her to comment, and, when I (finally!) got out and got home, I decided to give her a call.

She was legit. We talked for a while. Then I asked her to come and see me. That very weekend, she drove all the way up from Greensboro to visit.

It was so fucked up, and it still is. Everyone knew that I was in the hospital, how horrible of shape I was in, and, of everyone, here's this woman that doesn't even know me, willing to come so far out of nowhere to take care of me. That's a keeper.

We hung out for a few days. She went home, and I had to spend time with the doctors. Then I went down to see her, and I haven't really left.

47. Meeting and Marrying Jennifer

A month later, I asked her to marry me. I didn't really know why at that point, only that it felt right. I had a good instinct about her that I hadn't had before.

The next March, we got married. I'm hoping the third time's a charm.

Jennifer's true to her word. That's hard to find. She takes care of me. Takes me to the doctor, reads up on everything that gets wrong with me and studies it. She's really stepped up and helped me out, and I've never gotten that from any other women I'd married or gotten close with.

The point is, lots of people cheered for New Jack, held up signs for him, bought him drinks and drugs, and did all kinds of things for him. But she doesn't really think about New Jack. She loves me for who I am, away from the character. New Jack's OK, but she knows Jerome—and that's who she wants to be with.

48

Injuries

If you're trying to think of all the things you *don't* want to hear from anyone in the medical field, the words "Oh *shit!*" would probably be right near the top.

But yes, I've been there, and heard exactly that. Not that the circumstances weren't the dark epitome of extenuating. That dick-breaking kick from Jack Victory might have been the worst punishment my manhood has ever taken, but hardly the only one.

Stepping between the ropes for a match, I tripped and fell, and landed straight on a pole that held up the security rug, tearing right through my pants. OK, big deal. Wasn't like it would turn into a wardrobe malfunction or anything.

Flipping all over the ring, I kept seeing blood. Wet blood. Bright red blood. New blood, and more and more of it. I didn't see anyone else with color, and I hadn't gone to the blade just yet.

Then I saw a wet spot on my pants, right in a particular area. I reached down, and felt some blood flowing. Then the burning started.

I finished the match and headed to the back. That hole in my pants had grown, and so had the stain around it.

I pulled my pants down. Then I saw a newer, much larger, wider hole.

Right in the middle of my scrotum. Yeah, that's when the pain went through the roof and kept climbing.

"Oh fuck!" I was alternating screaming and thinking it, both at the highest volume. Then the medic walked in and echoed my sentiments.

Fortunately, the ambulance was already there. I got tossed on a stretcher, rolled out, and taken straight to the ER. Then they put me in stirrups like I was about to give birth, and sewed me right up. A week later, I was back in action.

In hindsight, I can laugh about things like that. But not all my injuries ended up light, and not all of them healed up so quickly. Or at all.

I'm proud of the scars on my face, just like a veteran's proud of his injuries from war. These will go with me to my grave; I'm not sure if anything could be done about them, but I wouldn't do anything anyway. I *always* cut myself (no one else ever did it for me), and sometimes I ended up with hack jobs that made the gashes I left on Mass Transit seem like nothing. I used pizza cutters, surgical scalpels, all kinds of shit. Sometimes I'd cut myself so deep I'd have flesh sticking out, and I'd have to get some scissors and cut it off. Then I'd freak people out by putting pennies in the lines on my head.

Anytime I bladed myself at a show, I always tried to do it so the fans wouldn't see it. It didn't always work.

"New Jack, you got a bleed!" I heard a guy yell in the middle of one show. I handed him the knife, my blood all over it, and he put it in his pocket. Probably the greatest souvenir in wrestling history!

Once I was in the ring, swinging a chain around like I was some sort of wild man or something. Showing just how tough New Jack could be, I slammed it on the mat.

Then I paid dearly. It bounced right back up—straight into my mouth. Almost everything in there shattered. My mouth was full of little chips and powder. I couldn't get to a dentist for about three days. When I finally did, I had almost all of my teeth capped, and then went right back to wrestling.

I've broken my leg at least three times, and ankle surgery will probably keep me from ever running again. I broke my elbow really badly once, and it still gives me all kinds of trouble. My back's shot to shit. Not that I didn't expect all of that. I had to take some breaks from my writing and editing of this book from getting hospitalized a few times.

All of that hurts like hell, but not all the time. There's nothing there that's so bad that I can't handle it.

I think I've been diagnosed with thirty

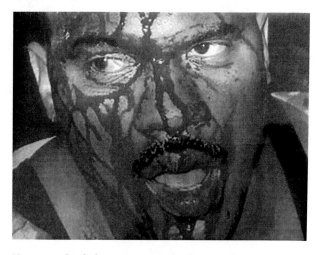

I'm proud of the scars on my face. I always cut *myself*—nobody ever did it for me.

195

concussions, which probably means I've had about twice that. I get head-aches all the time, and I'm on enough sleep medications to fill a pharmacy chain. Sometimes I take so much that I sleep all day and wake up at sun-down, then have some breakfast. My vision's never going to come all the way back and it jumps around a lot, which makes it tough for me to get a strong prescription for my glasses.

Right after the Grimes fall that permanently screwed my eyesight, I went to a brain institute to get an MRI. They found some stuff wrong, but told me they couldn't really study it until after I was dead. I didn't want any part of that, but I'm pretty sure if I were to let them study it, they'd find some spots, and probably some other signs, of some degenerative brain issue.

I've never liked taking medication, but I'm on some anti-psychotic meds right now. My temper shortens pretty quickly sometimes. That's a common thing with brain injuries: they make your tolerance level close to zero. Aside from the meds, there's really nothing that can be done right now.

My wife's pretty good at dealing with this. She'll notice me getting upset, and ask me if I'm agitated. I'm always like, "Yeah, can you tell?" She can. Sees right through this, and tells me to go in a room and lie down in the dark.

That helps. If it doesn't work, sometimes I'll mix some Xanax into a nice drink to chill out.

Here's a really tough part to tell. My memory's really screwed up, especially the short-term stuff. Writing this book has given me all sorts of trouble. If I try to strain my brain to look to the past, I'll go crazy. I've had to stop this book and start again so many times because I feel myself starting to slip. Maybe someday I'll have to rely on this book to remember New Jack's career in the ring—but I hope not.

Epilogue

How the fuck did I get here? How did this all happen?

How did I go from needing to be convinced to even *try* wrestling to almost dying for it? To almost handing it my life and health on a silver tray? I started out not even wanting to wrestle, and it ended up becoming my life, more so than it probably should have.

How? I've asked myself that before, and probably will again, and eventually have enough different answers to write another volume of this book. That's not the point. The point is, it did. And now I have to look at what's left.

I lost part of my sight, and it'll never come back. I almost died more times from drug use than I'll ever be aware of. I'm in pain right now, and if that particular affected area stops hurting, something else will surely start very soon after.

But regret? Never. Not me. There's no secret to keep from dwelling on the past, but if you do, wrestling's not the right world for you—though granted, it isn't the right world for most people.

Yeah, there are a few things that I wish hadn't happened. Of course, there's the Danbury fall with Grimes. That will always fuck with me—if he or I had just fallen about half a foot to one side or another, or if the table had broken differently, or if I'd been standing next to him when we fell, or if one of a ton of other things had happened, I'd still see great out of both eyes and not have come *this close* to ending everything myself. But I came back and went as hardcore as ever for almost two full decades afterward. I can be proud of that.

And yes, after almost two decades, I finally started to wish that the mess with Gypsy Joe hadn't happened. I don't regret it and I'm not going to say I was wrong, but it shouldn't have happened. He was stupid to get in the ring to begin with, but I beat the shit out of an old man. If I'd swung one of those weapons a little harder or aimed a few inches elsewhere, I could have killed that old man. I got pissed off and I wasn't going to let him handle me, but I shouldn't have gone that far to a guy about a hundred years old. Now, if he *wasn't* old enough to be my dad, I'd be bragging about it at the top of my lungs, like I feel I've earned the right to do with most of the other fights you've read about here, and many of the ones you haven't.

Wrestling's been in my life for decades, and I'll never be out of it. Not when my body and mind keep me sitting in the audience. Not even after my eulogy's read—and one of my brothers or sisters from the squared circle might just be the speaker there!—I'll live for quite a while in wrestling's memories.

What I did in wrestling was what I wanted to do. What, do you really think that if I'd ever said to a promoter, "Hey, could I *not* dive off a balcony tonight? How about if I go a while without having staples planted in my forehead?," any one of them would have ever refused? Of course not, not even Paul E. People can't force you to go that far. You do it because it's your job, even if you have to write your own rules sometimes.

Wrestling didn't wreck me, or steal my life. I allowed it. I opened the door and welcomed it in. And I think I did OK. I look at what I did for wrestling, and what it did for me. What would I have done if I'd said no to Melvin a few more times that day in Georgia so many years ago?

I used to drive trucks for a while, and I thought I'd do that. I studied to be a gym teacher in college, so I might have stayed there, and maybe done pretty well. Or you never know—maybe I'd have stayed in the drug-selling business, run into the wrong people, and ended up not getting away at all. You can't know everything, and there are just some things you don't have to know at all.

I've seen guys less talented, or at least less devoted to the business, get into bigger leagues than ECW, and enjoy the financial benefits, and, yes, that has pissed me off. I've held onto that for a while, maybe made it work for me sometimes, like using it to kick up some aggression all over my next opponent. But I've got too much to do to worry about that anymore.

For a guy who never made it into the WCW or WWE, and might not have been able to adapt to them anyway, I went a hell of a lot farther than many people who did. I find that out when people line up to meet me at awards shows, call me to do interviews, or send me plane tickets to fly across the country for a one-show appearance. If I've been out of the full-time business for over a decade and these things still happen so often, it means I did something right, and that there's a ton of people who still think so.

And yes, I still have some rules to stick by at those shows. If I get asked to wrestle again, and the money's good enough, I'll do it—but I don't lie down for the newbies. I'll advise them, mentor them, that's a blast and that's fine, but they're not going to pin New Jack. I've put too much time in the business to lie down for some local guy just starting out. Now, if I'm working with a fellow ECW frat brother, it might be a different story.

It's not easy being New Jack, and it was never easy being Jerome, long before wrestling was ever around. But you keep trying. Like with my kids. My relationship with them hasn't always been great, and with their moms, it's sometimes been even worse, but I do what I can for them, and with them. I'm still trying to fix the wrongs there, but parenting's the most inexact of sciences. You always try to get things right with your kids, or you're not a father at all. With everything I've ever been or will be called, off on the dad mark will never be one of them.

You've heard me mention not giving a fuck several times throughout this piece, and it probably came across wrong. When I say that, it doesn't always mean something hurtful. It's not that I'm looking at someone or some situation as a negative. Most of the time, it just means that I try not to worry too much about the past. I don't think about the times where I failed, got screwed over, couldn't get the hell out of my own way. I've got far too much baggage back there to let that bother me anymore.

I made it farther than most do, especially in a business like wrestling. A hell of a lot farther than anyone thought I ever would. My buddies that I robbed a jewelry store with, and the people in the cells next to me when the system made me pay. The people that I hunted down. Even ones that stood next to me while we were training, and watched me work the small crowds. Those that were down in Atlanta, telling me I'd never make it anywhere when I became a wrestling star, who are probably still there, badmouthing me.

But I don't take myself too seriously, and I don't take my own word for it. I'll take the word of the young wrestlers I see at these shows, the ones who let me know how much they cheered for me when they were kids, and how they still watch me today. I flip through my scrapbook and see the fan mail that I've gotten from people in prison, saying that I've inspired them. I've gotten letters from Europe, telling me about being the guy that got people interested in American culture to begin with.

I still get messages all over social media. Words from people who tell me that they watched me wrestle as kids, and now cheer for me as adults. People that I've inspired to go into wrestling. Promoters that fly me across the country to make my face the biggest on the event promotional poster, for a show called *New Jack City*, in 2019—over a decade after I first retired. The kids that come up to me at autograph shows and say, "I was too young to see you wrestle, but I've seen you on the Internet. You're still my favorite." Anyone would like hearing those words. They get more flattering all the time.

You know what? I guess I do give a fuck after all!

Index

Index